# Practical Recording

## Music On Mac OS X

Uwe G Hoenig

smt

# Practical Recording 6

## Music On Mac OS X

Also in this series and available from **smt**:

*Practical Recording 1: Microphones*
*Practical Recording 2: Pro Tools*
*Practical Recording 3: Cubase SX/SL*
*Practical Recording 4: Rhythm Programming (second edition)*
*Practical Recording 5: Surround Sound*
*Practical Recording 7: Reason*
*Practical Recording 8: Logic 6*

Printed in the United Kingdom by MPG Books, Bodmin

Published by SMT, an imprint of Sanctuary Publishing Limited, Sanctuary House, 45-53 Sinclair Road, London W14 0NS, United Kingdom

www.sanctuarypublishing.com

First published in Germany under the title *Musik Mit Mac OS X*, PPVMEDIEN GmbH, 2003. Text © Uwe G Hoenig 2003

ISBN: 1-84492-060-7

# CONTENTS

# CD CONTENTS

The accompanying CD contains various demo versions of applications and plug-ins as well as a variety of shareware and freeware and a basic stock of samples provided by Best Service to help you and your Mac make beautiful music together. Here's a breakdown of the CD contents:

## Demo Versions
### Effects

- **Native Bundle Demo 'Install.sit'** – Demo versions of the Native Bundle plug-ins from TC Works.

- **'Prosoniq' Folder** – Demo versions of various Prosoniq plug-ins.

- **'PSP' Folder** – Demo versions of various plug-ins from PSP Audioware.

- **'Trasher2_Demo.sit'** – Demo version of reFX's Trasher effects.

- **'vbox_1_1_trial.sit'** – Demo version of the multi-effects plug-ins from Bias Inc.

### Tone Generators

- **'reFX' Folder** – Demo versions of various tone generators from reFX.

- **'Tassman 3.0.2 Demo Install'** – Demo version of a modular physical-modelling synthesiser from AAS.

- **'TERAMacDemoX'** – Demo version of Tera, a modular synthesiser from VirSyn.

- **'VSTiHost3.01XDemo.sit'** – Demo version of a simple host program for VST instruments and effects.

### Sample Editors

- **'Amadeus II (US).sit'** – Demo version of Hairersoft's sample editor.

- **'MellodyneDemo.1.5.2.sit'** – Demo version of the sample editor from Celemony.

- **'peak_32_trial_g4_nd.sit'** – Demo version of the Peak sample editor from Bias (for G4 Macs only).

- **'peak_32_trial_nd.sit'** – Demo version of Peak for G3 Macs.

- **'SPARK XL Demo Install.sit'** – Demo version of TC Works' sample editor.

### Sequencers

- **'deck_3_5_trial'** – Demo version of Bias's Deck audio sequencer.

- **'InstallReason25DemoMacOSX.sit'** – Demo version of Reason from Propellerhead Software.

- **'LiveDemo203.sit'** – Demo version of Ableton Live, an audio sequencer.

## Shareware/Freeware/Donationware

- **'audacity-mac-1.0.0.sit'** – Audacity, a free open-source sample editor.

- **'Claw_1.0.sit'** – reFX's free synth.

- **'Granted' Folder** – Contains three free MIDI utilities.

- **'NorthPole™ VST OS X.sit'** – The free filter plug-in North Pole from Prosoniq.

- **'PSPvmVST'** – A free level-measurement plug-in from PSP Audioware.

- **'Smartelectronix' Folder** – Contains eight freeware or donationware plug-ins developed by the Smartelectronix community.

## Samples

This folder contains a selection of samples to get you started making music with Mac OS X. These samples can be used with any audio sequencer or software sampler.

Have fun browsing the CD!

# ABOUT THIS BOOK

*Practical Recording 6: Music On Mac OS X* is an introduction to making music with computers in general and the Mac and Mac OS X in particular. It contains an informed round-up of the current possibilities, detailed breakdowns of currently available audio and MIDI hardware, a host of technical details explained in jargon-free terms, guides to using the various applications designed for music production work, and describes how to go about arranging, mixing and mastering. In short, if all you've ever done in the past with your Mac is lay out catalogues, edit images or create pie charts, this book will provide you with a solid foundation from which to make music with Mac OS X, as well as give you some ideas for further avenues to explore.

The Internet plays an important role in this book, since it's a useful source of information, programs, updates and drivers, while it also provides an environment for making music collectively and serves as a platform for the distribution and publication of music. However, an Internet connection isn't absolutely necessary to enjoy this book as the accompanying CD contains a wealth of demo versions of the most important programs, as well a collection of shareware and freeware to get you started.

# ABOUT THE AUTHOR

Uwe G Hoenig has been involved with electronic music and studio technology for over 20 years, making music on computers ever since the days of the Atari 1040.

Hoenig was an early believer in the possibilities of computer-based music production and software-based tone generation and has mastered a wide range of applications and techniques over the years. A firm believer in the Mac's unequalled capacity for music-making, Hoenig lives in Freiburg, where he creates music with his iBook. He has published several specialist books on music and works as a freelance editor and author for German music magazine *KEYS*.

# INTRODUCTION

Working on the Mac opens up a whole world of creative possibilities for making music. On the one hand, the computer can serve as the equivalent of a multitrack tape recorder, allowing you to create, edit and play back audio recordings, while on the other it can be used to create sounds, taking on the role of traditional musical instruments. With the right software and speakers, for instance, the Mac can create a fairly realistic representation of a grand piano. You'll need to connect a keyboard before you can play it, of course, but once you've done that, the Mac is capable not only of generating the sounds but also of recording them at the same time. Naturally the piano is only one of a multitude of instruments that can be imitated in this way, and of course you're not restricted to emulating real instruments this way; like a synthesiser, the Mac can be used to create the type of futuristic sounds that can be produced only electronically.

**The Mac's ability to make music depends entirely on the applications that are running on it**

In this way, material is gathered take by take and track by track, then edited (if necessary) and arranged before being mixed down to stereo, perhaps, or to surround 5.1. Mixing involves finding the right balance between the various voices and instruments, placing them in the stereo or surround image, and trying to achieve the best overall sound so that you have just the right amount of bass and a transparent, undistorted treble. It's also at the mixing stage that effects and processes, such as echo and reverb, are introduced.

Once you have enough songs for an entire CD, you'll have to decide on the order in which they'll appear, and then you'll need to match their volume levels, ensuring that each begins cleanly and that any fade-outs are smooth, and this kind of work comes under the general heading of *mastering*. Here, too,

working on the Mac can make things very straightforward, as there's Mac-compatible software available to perform anything from sonic microsurgery to a radical facelift on the recorded material.

In short, the computer is a powerful and flexible musical tool, and making music with it is a broad subject comprising a number of different disciplines. In the course of a single production, you may well find yourself acting as composer, arranger, performer, sound designer, producer, recording engineer and mix engineer, while all the time playing the fundamental role of systems administrator. But don't worry; after all, you have this book!

*Practical Recording 6: Music On Mac OS X* contains everything you need to know to begin making music with the Mac. It explains all of the technical aspects of music production you'll encounter as well as the various steps and disciplines that this involves, outlining the different demands of various music genres. It also gives you an idea of the pros and cons of various methods of working, as well as introducing you to some of the hardware and software applications designed to assist with particular tasks. By the time you've reached the end, you should know enough about the subject, and have a good enough idea of the Mac's music-making potential, to be able to choose your own working methods and select the most appropriate tools for your own needs.

Naturally, there's not enough space in a book of this nature for an exhaustive examination of each subject. For those of you who do wish to study particular subjects in greater detail, the Appendix contains a list of links to Internet sites where each subject can be investigated further.

# 1 THE FUNDAMENTALS

Let's start off with an introduction to the concepts behind and terminology used in computer-based music production. This chapter is designed to provide readers who, instead of reading the book from cover to cover, prefer to dive straight into areas of relevance with a handy source of reference for those times when they encounter unfamiliar ideas or terminology.

## Beating The Jargon

If your experience of recording, synthesisers and music production as a whole has until now been rather, you're about to encounter a host of new terms, and you'll probably find it easier to understand the plethora of unfamiliar expressions you're about to come across than the complex ideas that underlie them. But don't worry! You don't need to commit each of these terms to memory; all the terms of real importance are repeated so often throughout this book that they'll soon become part of your working vocabulary.

## Digital Audio

In order to make music with your Mac, you'll first have to understand what a sound wave is. Of course, if you already know what the terms *audio resolution* and *sample rate* mean, you can skip the next section. The rest of you, brace yourselves; it's time to learn about the 'birds and bees' of digital audio.

In the natural world, we experience sound in the form of variations in air pressure caused by waves of compression and rarefaction radiating outwards from a sound source. As the waves move further from the source, they lose energy due to friction, and the sound grows fainter. The classic analogy of this phenomenon is that of ripples forming when you throw a stone into

a still pond. The purest form of oscillation is a sine wave, which has no overtones and sounds very much like the sound produced by a tuning fork.

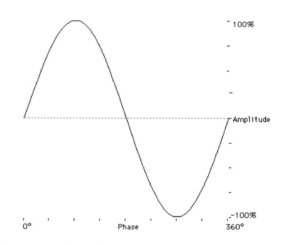

**Representation of a sine wave**

Before sound waves can be processed or stored electronically, they must first be transformed into an electrical signal using a microphone or other transducer. The resulting signal is described as 'analogue' because the variations in voltage of the signal are directly analogous to the variations in air pressure of the sound. Indeed, every increase in air pressure brings about a corresponding increase in the voltage, and every decrease in air pressure causes a corresponding decrease in the voltage such that, if you were to superimpose a graph describing the fluctuations in air pressure upon a graph describing those of electrical voltage, you'd find that the two curves were identical. They would also be exactly *in phase* – ie the voltage changes instantly, without delay, in response to changes in the air pressure.

There's plenty of electronic equipment that exists for the purpose of manipulating analogue signals – through amplification, for example, or the addition of effects – but this kind of manipulation doesn't alter the two basic characteristics of an analogue signal: that it is continuously variable (ie free from jumps) and that it traces the variations in air pressure of the original sound without incurring any delay. The continuous nature of an analogue signal is its defining characteristic and is also the greatest merit of analogue technology.

Computers, on the other hand, employ *digital* technology, and digital signals are not continuous. Where an analogue signal can be thought of as a line graph, a digital signal is more like a bar chart, being made up of a multitude of discrete values. Only when these values are converted back into an analogue signal does a continuous, curved waveform re-emerge. However, the advantages of working with digital signals lie in the wide variety of ways in which they can be manipulated and how easily they can be stored. The problem with digital signals, however, is that, because they consist of discrete integer values, any variation in their values is displayed not as a curve but as a series of tiny steps, which means that they can never be anything more than an approximate rendering (albeit a close one) of the original sound wave.

The number of steps by which an analogue signal is measured each second by a digital-to-analogue converter is known as the *sampling rate*, and this is directly related to the accuracy of the digital signal. If the sampling rate is too low, rapid fluctuations in the waveform (ie its high-frequency content) won't be detected and inaccuracies will creep in, and the resulting sound will be dull and marred by distortion. The higher the sampling rate, the more accurately the higher frequencies will be reproduced.

The sampling rate of an audio CD is 44.1kHz (kiloHertz). In other words, the voltage is sampled – ie measured – 44,100 times each second to produce a signal consisting of the values that result from these measurements. According to a theorem developed by the mathematician Harry Nyquist, a sampling rate of 44.1kHz should be sufficient to capture all frequencies up to around 20,000Hz, which is theoretically the upper limit of human hearing.

While the standard CD sampling rate of 44.1kHz is currently the most common, DAT (Digital Audio Tape) and various sound cards sample at 48kHz, while DAT Long Play uses 32kHz and modern audio systems – such as audio DVD and the latest computer hardware – often use sampling rates of 96kHz or higher, capturing a much wider frequency range. Higher sampling rates also mean further benefits in the areas of signal processing and sound reproduction.

The quality of a digital audio signal can be expressed in terms of two values, the *sampling rate* and the *bit resolution* (or *word length*), the latter of which is the number of different values available to represent the amplitude. Since only integers (ie whole numbers) can be used to describe the amplitude of any given sample, the more integers are available in a signal, the closer the approximation to the original sound. Conversely, the fewer values are available, the coarser the approximation and the more distortion is present in the signal. Returning to the analogy of a bar chart, if the sampling rate is the horizontal resolution (ie the number of measurements per second), the word length is the vertical resolution (ie the precision of those measurements).

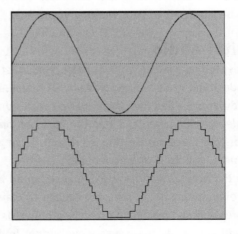

**The digital representation of a waveform is represented by steps, the breadth and height of which depend on the sampling rate and word length, respectively**

Since computers operate on the binary system, whereby numbers are represented using only two digits, 1 and 0, a word length of 16 bits (the CD standard) yields $2^{16}$ (ie 65,536) possible values to represent the signal amplitude.

DVD and other high-quality modern formats use a word length of 24 bits. Since the number of possible values doubles with each additional bit, a word length of 24 bits offers 16 million possible values to describe the amplitude of each sample, which represents a colossal improvement in resolution. Computers generally employ 32-bit floating-point arithmetic to realize this, but fortunately you don't need to concern yourself with this!

Each successive measurement of the amplitude is known as a *sample* or *sample word*, the terms *16-bit sample* and *24-bit samples* refer to samples with word lengths of 16 or 24 bits, respectively. Unfortunately, the word *sample* is also, more commonly, used to describe a complete digital recording, rather than one of the measurements of which it consists. If you 'sample' (ie record) a snare-drum hit at a sampling rate of 44.1kHz and the recording lasts two seconds, you'd have a 'sample' (in the more common meaning) consisting of 88,200 individual 'samples' (in the more technical sense outlined here). Of course, most of the time it's obvious which definition of the word is being used.

Although some people use the term 'audio resolution' as though it's synonymous with word length, it's actually determined by the sampling frequency and word length combined. These two concepts feature in a wide range of contexts, which is why it's important to understand their implications.

As we've seen, doubling the sampling rate doubles a recording's frequency range while at the same time doubling the load on the computer, since it needs to process twice the number of values in the same amount of time. However, increasing the word length of a recording from the CD standard of 16 bits to the new standard of 24 increases the amplitude resolution by a factor of $2^8$ (ie 256), but in terms of storage space it requires only a third as much again. This type of calculation can come in useful when, for example, your computer's CPU is nearing overload or you're running short of space on your hard disk.

## Audio Formats

Audio data can be stored in a number of different file formats on your computer's hard disk. The most commonly encountered format on the Mac is AIFF (Audio Interchange File Format), originally introduced by Apple, while Windows-based systems use WAV format.

The two formats are in fact very similar, supporting a variety of word lengths and sampling rates, with files in each format bearing a header containing all the relevant information along with data concerning such things as the locations of any loop points. Practically all software applications can handle files in both AIFF and WAV formats and may even support others, such as SDII (Sound Designer II), which was once a common format on the Mac. Even though considerably larger word lengths and higher sampling rates are now used, AIFF and WAV files in 44.1kHz/16-bit audio resolution represent the norm and are fine for most purposes.

Both AIFF and WAV formats store audio data in as much detail as the sampling frequency and word length will allow, which means there's no loss of audio resolution or fidelity. A one-minute AIFF or WAV file of CD-quality (16-bit/44.1kHz) stereo will take up around 10MB of space on a hard disk. However, there are other formats out there that are designed to reduce the amount of storage space required by audio material (ie *lossy* formats), the most popular being MP3, the standard format for file exchange over the Internet as well as that used by modern digital players, such as Apple's iPod.

When audio data is stored in MP3 or the increasingly popular Ogg Vorbis (.ogg) format, it's first analysed and then a series of psychoacoustic algorithms are applied to 'thin out' the data without degrading the audio quality too noticeably. The more drastic this thinning process, the less data needs to be transmitted and the less space is required to store it. However, these compression/decompression algorithms, or *codecs*, do cause a loss of audio quality, and it depends on the application and the storage space or bandwidth available whether or not it makes sense to use them.

As with other formats, the quality of an MP3 file is primarily determined by the bit rate, which is measured in KBps (kilobits per second). MP3 files with a bit rate of 128KBps are one-tenth the size of the equivalent

WAV or AIFF files, which – considering that the loss in audio quality is negligible – makes it a very economical medium if bandwidth or storage space are at a premium. At the even higher rate of 160KBps, MP3 files are said to be indistinguishable from CDs in quality. At rates below 128KBps, however, the quality does fall off rather sharply, which is why their use is best confined to the Internet.

When processing audio, music and audio programs seldom employ codecs that introduce lossy compression, although they are generally capable of saving and opening (and converting) files in these formats. However, only very seldom do these applications work directly with MP3 files, almost invariably having AIFF or WAV as a standard file format.

## What Is MIDI And What Is It For?

At some point when making music with your computer, you're bound to be confronted not only with digital audio but also with digital data of a quite different nature called MIDI.

MIDI stands for Musical Instrument Digital Interface. Why, you might ask, is such an interface necessary? Well, if you remember the example cited earlier – whereby a software module was being used to generate the sounds of a grand piano and a piano-style keyboard without a tone generation section of its own to input the notes – MIDI is the protocol via which the keyboard and application communicate.

The MIDI protocol contains all the performance data generated by the playing of keys at the keyboard, as well as the use of sustain and volume pedals and pitch-bend and modulation wheels. The data by which it operates consists of a series of messages that translate something like this: 'The note C3 has just been depressed hard [a value between 0 and 127 is used to quantify the velocity of the key]. Now G3 has been pressed, rather less hard. Now the sustain pedal has been pressed. Now the two keys have been released. Now the sustain pedal has been released,' and so on.

In other words, MIDI passes information describing a musical performance from one device to another, making it possible for a keyboard and software or hardware synth to communicate, providing a language that all devices can employ and understand, even though they might be of different makes. Originally introduced in 1983 to allow the musical instruments of different manufacturers to communicate, it quickly became a universal standard and revolutionised the market for electronic musical instruments. It's now difficult to find any item of music hardware that doesn't sport the familiar five-pin MIDI connector, and these days, as well as serving as a communication protocol for keyboards and synths, MIDI is also used to control mixing desks, lighting equipment and a host of other devices.

One such device – and a particularly important one – is the computer, which was soon being used for the recording, editing and playback of MIDI messages. The principle is very simple: during recording, MIDI messages are stored on the computer's hard disk or in its RAM (Read Only Memory), along with data concerning the moment at which they were received. When the messages are played back, the same (unedited) signals are transmitted from the computer to the synth or application at precisely the same intervals of time (ie at the same rhythm and tempo) as during the original performance. To the synth or application, it makes no difference whether the messages are being transmitted live from the keyboard or played back subsequently by the computer; the messages – and, therefore, the music that results – are the same in each case.

It is very important to understand that MIDI data consists solely of messages describing the actions of the performer and, as such, is completely different from

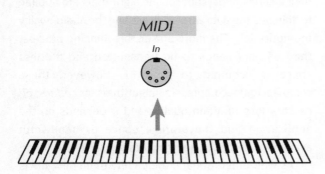

**MIDI is the means by which the software knows which notes on the keyboard have been pressed, how hard and for how long**

audio data. With either, of course, it's possible to record anything from a single note to an entire piano sonata; the only difference is that the audio data stores the actual *sounds*, whereas the MIDI data merely contains *information*, and the volume of data generated by the two types of recording is consequently very different. A CD-quality digital stereo recording, for example, takes up 10MB of hard-disk space per minute, while MIDI data relating to the same performance is unlikely to take up more than a few kilobytes.

There's another area where MIDI scores over audio. Whereas with an audio recording the notes played are inseparable from the instrument playing them, with MIDI the performance can be recorded on any MIDI instrument and played back on a synth set to reproduce the sound of an organ, banjo or kazoo, or a whole host of different instrumental sounds. Similarly, you could play back a techno arrangement and substitute the original synth sounds with those of a string quartet or brass band!

```
POSITION          STATUS   CHA   NUM UAL LENGTH/INFO
------------- Anfang der Liste -------------
  1  1  1    1 C-Press 1          0
  1  1  1    1 C-Press 1          0
  1  1  1    1 C-Press 1          0
  1  1  1    1 C-Press 1          0
  1  1  1    1 Program 1      -   0     Grand Piano
  1  1  1    1 Note    1    B2  80      _ _  1   0
  1  1  1    1 Control 1      7 127 Volume
  1  1  1    1 Control 1      7 127 Volume
  1  1  1    1 Control 1      7 127 Volume
  1  1  2    1 Note    1    F2  80      _ _  1   0
  1  1  3    1 Note    1    G3  80      _ _  1   0
  1  1  3    1 Note    1   G#4  80      _ _  1   0
  1  1  4    1 Note    1   C#2  80      _ _  1   0
  1  2  2    1 Note    1    C2  80      _ _  1   0
  1  2  2    1 Note    1   G#4  80      _ _  1   0
  1  2  4    1 Note    1    G3  80      _ _  1   0
  1  4  1    1 Note    1   F#4  80      _ _  1   0
  1  4  2    1 Note    1   C#3  80      _ _  1   0
------------- Ende der Liste ----------------
```

**MIDI data comprises information about the performance but never the sounds themselves**

While MIDI was originally designed to connect physically separate hardware instruments and devices, the protocol is being used increasingly these days for exchanging messages between different software applications or program modules within a single computer. In either case, the principle is the same.

Whereas a few years ago tone generators such as synthesisers and samplers took the form of external hardware, today, thanks to the greatly increased power of modern processors, these kinds of devices are often nothing more than software modules running inside the computer itself and, as such, are fully MIDI-compatible.

The terms *synthesisers* here could refer to a number of devices:

- A keyboard instrument with a large number of buttons, rotary controls and sliders;

- A hardware rack module containing the same electronics and controls as the first example but with no keyboard;

- A piece of software, visible only on the computer monitor.

Although the sound produced by all three might be identical, the most obvious difference between the third example – the software synth – and the other two types is that software instruments have no knobs or sliders that you can operate with your hands. This is generally not a problem, however, since your MIDI keyboard will usually be connected to the computer, and it will generally be equipped with knobs, buttons and sliders of its own that you can use to change the synth's parameters, which is a lot easier than entering values using the computer keyboard or mouse. It's also possible to connect a hardware controller (a device resembling a mixing console) and assign its controls to the same parameters. Hardware controllers will be covered in greater detail later in the book.

# Synthesisers

Synthesisers are electronic devices used to produce sounds – ie they are electronic musical instruments. The first synths, designed back in the '60s, were few and far between and took the form of enormous control panels with vast arrays of knobs and cables that were every bit as imposing as the telephone switchboards of the period.

Nowadays, switchboards are far smaller and less obtrusive and employ digital rather than analogue technology, and synths have undergone a similar development. First of all they were transformed from huge panels into devices that more resembled musical instruments, although they still employed analogue technology. Then digital technology took over, they became more compact and numerous new systems of tone generation were invented, increasing the range and sophistication of the sounds they were capable of producing.

One of the latest developments is that of the software synth, which incorporates exactly the same range of functions and exactly the same algorithms as popular hardware synths, and therefore produces exactly the same sounds. This is miniaturisation taken to extremes, the synth itself having ceased to exist altogether as a physical entity.

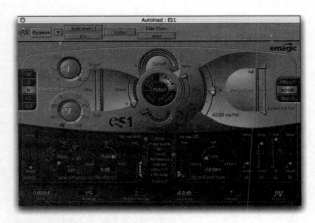

**Emagic's ES1 software synth**

As their name suggests, synthesisers were originally designed to reproduce artificially (ie synthesise) the sounds of traditional instruments. However, it was quickly discovered that they were capable of producing sounds and sound effects that were more interesting than their seldom-convincing impersonations of other instruments.

Musically, synths are used most commonly in one of two ways: monophonically (ie one note at a time) as an alternative to the lead guitar, handling solos and riffs; or polyphonically (ie several notes at once) to fill in the harmonies, in which case they play a similar background role to a Fender Rhodes piano or

a string section. They also operate on a variety of different principles, as described below.

## Subtractive Synthesis

This is the classic process of tone generation that the early analogue synths were based on, and it's still popular today. The process isn't limited to analogue devices, and many hardware and software digital synths use it as well.

With subtractive synthesis, one or more oscillators are used to produce what is generally an unchanging soundwave that's rich in overtones, and there are usually a variety of different waveforms provided, including sawtooth, triangle and square. With each of these waveforms, the name indicates the shape of the wave.

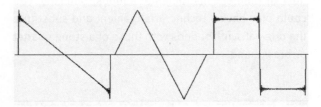

**The classic synth waveforms. L-r: sawtooth, triangular and square**

These waveforms sound much like they look:

- **Sawtooth Wave** – with its sharp edges, this waveform has a very penetrating sound that cuts through the mix. The tone colour is bright and rich in overtones, making it suitable for synthesising the sound of rasping brass instruments or for aggressive electronic sounds.

- **Square Wave** – This has a timbre more like that of woodwind instruments. It's not as rich in overtones, but it's nonetheless very distinctive.

- **Triangular Wave** – This waveform is less jagged than the sawtooth and has a milder timbre, something like that of a flute.

- **Sine Wave** – This waveform is quite different from the other forms, since it has a mathematically pure oscillation and no overtones whatsoever. More complex waveforms can be produced by combining sine waves of different pitches and amplitudes, whereas a single sine wave has a rather dull sound lacking in character.

Synthesisers are capable not only of reproducing these waveforms but also of reshaping them, sometimes radically. One of the most important reshaping devices is the *filter*, which removes overtones from the raw waveform, causing the sawtooth wave, for example, to sound progressively less bright the more the filter is used. In other words, the filter removes elements of the signal, which is why this type of synthesis is described as being *subtractive*.

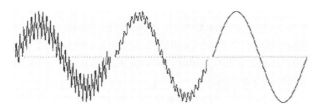

**A low-pass filter gradually removes overtones until only a sine wave remains**

As the overtone content of the signal is reduced or removed altogether, the bright sound of the sawtooth wave gradually gives way to something duller. This involves a process known as *low-pass filtering*, whereby the high frequencies of a signal are attenuated (ie reduced in intensity) while its low-frequency content passes undiminished. Of course, it's possible to get filters that do the exact opposite, and these *high-pass filters* attenuate the low frequencies and allow the high frequencies to pass unaffected, creating a thinner, more nasal sound. When both types of filter are combined, frequencies above and below a particular band are attenuated, while frequencies within the band are allowed to pass undiminished. This is known as *band-pass filtering*.

By now you're probably looking at the treble and bass controls on your hi-fi and wondering whether the low- and high-pass filters of a sequencer have a similar effect on the audio signal. They don't. These hi-fi tone controls are really just a basic equaliser. You can use them to make the low or high frequencies a little louder or softer, but they're incapable of removing these frequencies altogether.

The filters of a synthesiser have a rather more radical effect on the signal. When you turn up a low-pass filter, the sound becomes steadily duller until all you can hear is a rumble in the bass before the sound eventually disappears altogether, whereas, when you turn up a high-pass filter, the bass is steadily removed, the sound becoming more nasal until all that remains is a high-frequency hiss, which eventually disappears. The equaliser on your hi-fi can't do this.

High- and low-pass filters normally offer a parameter that determines the point at which the filter begins to take effect (known as the *corner*, *roll-off* or *cut-off frequency*, or the *3dB down point*), and this parameter is one of the most important in subtractive synthesis. Any frequencies that fall above this level (in the case of a low-pass filter) or below it (with a high-pass filter) are progressively attenuated.

Another very important parameter is *filter resonance*. This parameter has the effect of emphasising the frequencies around the corner frequency. The higher the resonance of the filter, the greater this area is emphasised until, when the resonance is turned all the way up, the filter begins to whistle. This is known as *self-oscillation*.

**Synth control panel displaying controls for filter corner frequency and resonance, the two critical parameters in subtractive synthesis**

The Resonance control can be used to emphasise particular overtones and also to create interesting dynamic effects, such as filter sweeps, while it's also responsible for many of the sounds typically associated with synths. Taken together, the Filter and Resonance controls of a synth offer a simple yet highly effective means of shaping the sound, which is one of the reasons why subtractive synthesis is still such a popular means of tone shaping.

Most of a synth's other components and parameters play a subordinate role in subtractive synthesis. Many of them are concerned with modulation, which is a means of performing automatically what you'd otherwise have to do by hand – making the sound alternately louder and quieter, for example, as though you were moving the Volume knob. Envelopes and LFOs are typical modulation sources.

An envelope generator applies a one-off modulation pattern to the signal each time a key is pressed. It can be used to control the volume, determining the rate at which the sound grows louder when the key is first pressed and how quickly it dies away when the key is released. Meanwhile, a second envelope generator might be applying a different modulation pattern to the filter so that the timbre gradually becomes duller the longer the note is sustained.

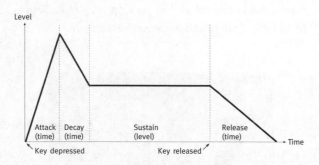

**Envelopes begin when the key is depressed and modulate one of several parameters automatically**

An LFO (Low-Frequency Oscillator) creates a similar effect, except that, rather than being a one-off event, the modulation pattern it produces is *cyclic*, which means that it's a waveform like that produced by any other oscillator except that it operates at a

considerably lower frequency. Typical applications for periodic LFO modulation are vibrato (pitch modulation), wah-wah effects (filter modulation) and tremolo (volume modulation).

## Additive Synthesis

As its name implies, additive synthesis is the opposite of subtractive synthesis. Whereas with subtractive synthesis you start off with an overtone-rich sound and then remove parts of the overtone content using a filter, additive synthesis involves taking a sine wave (which has no overtones) and then creating the overtone pattern you want by adding other sine waves to it.

Complex waveforms are made up of *partials* comprising the fundamental (ie the first partial) and the overtones (the upper partials), and each partial is equivalent to a sine wave. Since any given waveform can be broken down into its constituent sine waves, it follows that, in theory, any sound can be recreated by combining sine waves of the correct pitch and amplitude.

In practice, things are rather more complex. If you wanted to synthesise a truly complex sound, such as a sentence of human speech, simply through the addition of sine waves, you'd need hundreds, if not thousands of oscillators, each with a constantly changing frequency and amplitude. Obviously, a device of such complexity would no longer resemble a musical instrument.

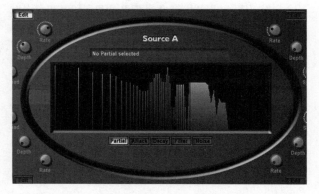

**A mixer for overtones. On an additive synthesiser, waveforms are created by setting the volume levels of each partial, allowing sounds to be shaped with great precision**

For this reason, commercial additive synthesisers offer a simplified form of additive synthesis known as *harmonic additive synthesis*, which uses a limited number (usually between 32 and 128) of sinusoidal oscillators confined in pitch to the notes of the harmonic series – in other words, to frequencies that are integer multiples of the fundamental frequency. If the frequency of the fundamental is f, the other oscillators will give 2f (the first harmonic), 3f (the second harmonic), 4f (the third harmonic) and so on, while inharmonic overtones – ie those whose frequencies are non-integer multiples of the fundamental frequency – are excluded. Nonetheless, it's possible to achieve a very wide palette of tone colours simply by varying the volume of the various harmonic overtones individually.

Synths that operate on the basis of additive synthesis are generally more complex and less intuitive than those that work by subtractive synthesis, which is doubtless why they're less popular, and also why you only ever come across digital models; analogue models would be too expensive to produce. Having said that, a very simple electro-mechanical form of additive synthesis underlies the good old Hammond organ, on which a great variety of timbres can be created by mixing sine waves, using the drawbars.

### Wavetable Synthesis

Typically, subtractive synthesis employs a few simple waveforms whose overtone content is attenuated – often quite drastically, but always in much the same way – by a filter, since a low-pass filter can only ever attenuate high frequencies, just as a high-pass filter can only ever attenuate low frequencies. Wavetable synthesis operates on much the same principle except

that, instead of simple waveforms, the oscillators generate what are called *wavetables*.

A wavetable comprises several different waveforms which, like the individual frames of a cartoon, represent the successive forms of a developing sound. These waveforms are arranged in a meaningful order to recreate realistically the various stages (attack, release, etc) through which the sound of a regular instrument passes. The 'frames' can be played either individually or in sequence. Depending on the wavetable selected and its constituent waveforms, it's possible to produce sound patterns using wavetable synthesis that would be impossible to achieve using a filter.

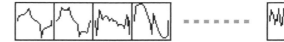

**In a wavetable, different waveforms are arranged in sequence**

Wavetable synthesisers can produce very vibrant digital sounds that are a useful complement to the sound palette of a normal subtractive synth. Of course, if you dispense with the idea of using multiple waveforms and rely on using just the filter to shape the sound, your wavetable synth can produce typical subtractive analogue sounds.

Wavetable synthesis was invented by the German engineer Wolfgang Palm, whose firm, PPG, produced wavetable synths in the '70s and '80s and marketed them worldwide. Today, wavetable synths – including a software version of the PPG bestseller Wave 2.2/3 – are primarily associated with the German manufacturer Waldorf.

**The Waldorf PPG 2.V is a software version of the classic PPG wavetable synthesiser**

## FM Synthesis

FM (Frequency Modulation) synthesis represents a fundamentally different approach to the creation of complex waveforms. It was invented in the '60s in the University of Stanford's Department of Computer Music by Professor Dr John Chowning and was later licensed to Yamaha, who developed the idea further before marketing it in the form of the legendary DX7, one of the most commercially successful synths of all time.

FM synthesis is more like additive than subtractive synthesis, since the overtone spectrum isn't obtained through filtering more complex waveform but rather by combining simpler ones. However, FM synthesis offers less control than normal additive synthesis, as you can't use it to adjust the amplitude of each individual overtone separately.

On the other hand, with FM synthesis it's possible to create a rich series of overtones from only two sine waves when the output of the first oscillator (known as the *modulator*) is fed into the modulation input of the second (the *carrier*). The frequencies of both oscillators are within the audio range, so the result is a normal audio signal. This process is exactly the same as vibrato, except that the LFO modulating the frequency of the audible oscillator to create vibrato has a frequency of only 3–5Hz.

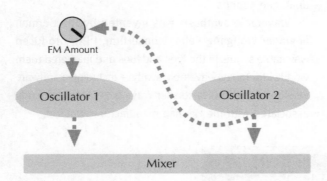

**With FM synthesis, one oscillator is used the modulate the frequency of a second**

With FM synthesis, since the frequencies of both oscillators are within the audio range, a lot of new overtones are produced instead of vibrato. The difference in pitch of the oscillators and the intensity of the modulation determines which actual overtones are produced; the greater the intensity, the richer and brighter the resulting sound.

Effects that are typically associated with filters, such as the gradual dulling of the sound produced by the low-pass filter, can be achieved via FM synthesis by altering the intensity of the frequency modulation so that, instead of modulating the filter, the envelope generator is used to control the intensity of the frequency modulation, producing effects such as the transition from a bright to a dull sound as the note is held. While the underlying principle might be very different from that of a low-pass filter, the resulting effect is similar.

What makes frequency modulation synthesis so versatile and powerful, but at the same time both unintuitive and unpredictable, is the fact that not just two but as many as four or even eight oscillators (depending on the model of synth) can be combined in different modulation configurations to create a wide variety of vibrant tone colours. Of course, the oscillators don't need to be stacked vertically; if combined horizontally, the signal of each is simply added to that of the next, in much the same way as the Hammond organ produces modulation. As more oscillators are combined, the number of possible permutations increases, with some stacked and others connected horizontally. A separate envelope generator is assigned to each of the digital sine-wave oscillators, the oscillator and envelope combining to create what's known as an *operator*.

One of the most popular sounds that can be recreated using FM synthesis is the bell-like Fender piano sound, but it can also produce some excellent wiry, dynamic clavinet and guitar sounds, crisp basses and a number of other sounds, both instrumental and those with no physical equivalent.

## Physical Modelling

This manner of synthesis involves a different and more specialised approach than any of the forms described so far. With physical modelling, the objective isn't to create a universal and versatile tone-generation architecture capable of producing as diverse a sound palette as possible. Instead, the objective of physical modelling is to imitate all the nuances of a particular type of instrument – strings or woodwind, for example – as realistically as possible, and the entire tone-generation architecture is optimised to achieve this one objective.

For this kind of tone generation to be successful, the way in which the instrument in question produces sound needs to be analysed in as much detail as possible. Here, each stage of sound production is analysed in turn, beginning with the actuator (ie the plectrum, hammer, bow or reed) and followed by the resonant body of the instrument (ie the body of a guitar or violin, the shaft of a flute or the combined tube and bell of a brass instrument). Each component that contributes to the sound of the instrument is examined in turn and described mathematically, and a set of equations and algorithms is then devised to recreate its behaviour.

**Actuator, tube and bell: the components of a clarinet model**

What's remarkable about physical-modelling synths isn't so much how close their synthesised sound is to that of the original instrument as the authenticity of their playing characteristics. For instance, it's even possible to overblow a flute created using physical modelling, and if the virtual air stream is too weak to cause the virtual column of air to vibrate, you hear the breath noise but no note, just as you would with the real instrument.

Physical-modelling synths have a relatively small sonic repertoire but are capable of creating extraordinarily life-like instrument sounds and can be used to produce highly expressive performances. Having said that, you can also produce weird and wonderful effects on them by entering extreme parameter values (to create a guitar with strings as thick as a tow rope, for example) or by combining

components in physically impossible ways to create instruments that have no physical counterpart, such as a plucked flute or a blown piano.

# Sampling

Along with subtractive synthesis, sampling is one of the most widely used forms of electronic tone generation. The term *sampling* refers to the recording, digitisation, storage and playback of sounds using the technology described earlier in the section on 'Digital Audio'. In effect, a sampler works in much the same way as a tape recorder or any other device used to record and play back sounds, but with two important differences: a sampler is capable of transposing a recording and of playing it back polyphonically.

Transposition is achieved by playing back the sampled sound at a different pitch by raising or lowering the speed of playback, much like playing a 33rpm record back at 45rpm raises the pitch of the original material. In theory, this allows you to play an entire melody with a single sample, but there are practical limits. For example, if you were to play back a sample an octave higher than its recorded pitch, its note length would be halved. Furthermore, a single sample of a grand piano isn't enough to reproduce realistically the full keyboard, so if you want to achieve an authentic rendering of an instrument, you'll need to use a technique known as *multisampling*. In the case of the grand piano, for example, this might involve taking samples every four notes across the entire keyboard to ensure that whatever sample is played back will never be more than a minor third (ie three semitones) from the original sample. In order to allow long notes to be played without gobbling up vast amounts of RAM or disk space, each sample contains a loop point, which keeps repeating for as long as the note is held. Depending upon the sound in question and the way it's being used, such a loop could be a few milliseconds or several seconds long.

Finding the best part of a sample to loop is a time-consuming business, as the transition from the end of the loop to the beginning has to sound as natural as possible. Any difference in volume between the beginning and end of the loop might not be noticed on the first pass, but as it loops back to the beginning there will be an annoying click.

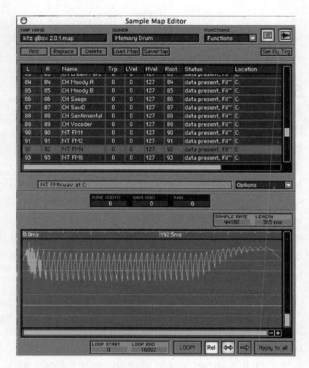

Reaktor's Sample Map Editor, which allows various samples to be assigned to different parts of the keyboard

Reason's NNXT sampler with a grand-piano multisample loaded

than synthetic imitations of the same sounds, but they have a tendency to sound sterile and lifeless, as each note has exactly the same characteristics each time it's played. Meanwhile, a synthetic rendering of the same instrument by a physical-modelling synth might not reproduce any one of its sounds with quite the same fidelity, yet it sounds more authentic and convincing as it captures the iridescence of the instrument and its changing nuances in live performance.

Another factor that distinguishes a sampler from a tape recorder is *polyphony*. Basically, polyphony describes a device's capacity for playing back the same sample (or multisamples) simultaneously at different pitches – in other words, to play chords. Similarly, it's possible to assign samples that are derived from different instruments to different parts of the keyboard, or to different channels, so that the same device can be used to play back piano, bass and drum samples simultaneously, in which case the device is described as being *multitimbral*. At least one sampler voice is required for each audible note.

Samplers are very good at imitating acoustic instruments and generally come equipped with vast libraries of sounds including grand pianos, strings and choirs and many other digitised acoustic sounds. When it comes to emulating acoustic instruments, they compare very favourably with physical-modelling synths.

However, both samplers and modelling synths have their pros and cons. Samplers might reproduce the transients and timbre of real instruments more accurately

Samplers are versatile workhorses for all types of music production, contributing a multitude of different instrument sounds and assuming the lion's share of responsibility for playing back drum and percussion sounds, while they're also suitable for drum loops, effects and atmospheric sounds. By transposing samples by an extreme amount, it's also possible to generate some interesting effects. In fact, if you have to choose, a sampler will probably turn out to be of more use than a synth for most applications; after all, you can always sample synth sounds if you need them, whereas a synth can't deputise for a sampler quite as easily.

In practice, the distinction between synths and samplers is less clear cut, as there's a great deal of overlap between the two devices. For example, samplers generally offer a filter, envelopes and LFOs to shape the sound – components typically associated

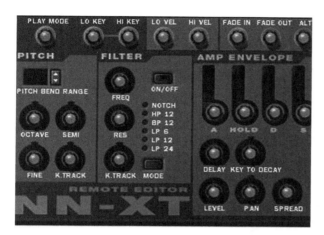

**A revealing close-up: typical synth functions are also encountered in samplers**

with synths. The only real difference lies in the fact that a sampler doesn't have oscillators with fixed waveforms, using instead samples loaded by the user.

The reverse is also true. Synth designers have been quick to appreciate the usefulness of sampling technology, and today there are many instruments on the market that offer a colourful hotchpotch of sampled waveforms as raw material for their filters, envelope generators and LFOs. And when it comes to imitating the sounds of acoustic instruments, these samples are often better than the simpler waveforms.

The difference between sample-based synths and straight samplers lies in the fact that users of the former generally can't use their own samples, at best being able only to supplement their basic stock of samples with those supplied by add-on modules. Such devices are obviously no substitute for real samplers, which you can use to record and use your own samples.

**Sample CDs And CD-ROMs**
The sound libraries you find bundled with most samplers are really little more than a starter pack, a collection that the manufacturers feel most users will be happy to use out of the box. However, today's music is so diverse, each branch seeking to set itself apart from its neighbours by developing a unique sonic style, and the dictates of fashion have created such a demand for new and distinctive sounds that a whole new industry has sprung up to provide each genre with new sound sets on an almost monthly basis. I'm not talking

here about standard sounds, such as grand piano, string and woodwind samples, but things like drum and synth loops that are created in response to popular demand and summarily fall out of fashion.

There's currently a huge variety of commercial sound libraries available on CD, ranging from trendy music-construction sets with sure-fire commercial appeal to high-quality collections of loops and instrument samples and even libraries of sounds and phrases recorded by large symphony orchestras and aimed at film-score composers.

Sample CDs and CD-ROMs provide additional raw material and tools for computer- or sampler-assisted music production, offering an enormous choice of sounds, rhythms, effects and atmospheres. As a result, it's seldom necessary these days to pack a mic and go off in search of new sounds to record. And sound libraries can also prove a rich source of inspiration, stimulating the imagination and acting as a catalyst for new ideas.

Since the DVD has failed so far to make any significant impact in this area, audio CDs and CD-ROMs are the data-storage media that dominate the sound-library market. Sample CDs, for instance, are normal audio CDs and can therefore be played by any standard CD player. They can contain any type of sound material and are generally very reasonably priced, costing £20–£60 per CD. Their advantage lies in the fact that they don't require a specific platform or device in order to be accessed, although they require you to do a considerable amount of work before you can use them; converting them first into a Mac- or sampler-compatible format, then cutting them to the correct lengths (in the case of typical instrument samples) and perhaps even inserting loop points can be a very time-consuming process.

CD-ROMs, on the other hand, are considerably more convenient to use. As a universal data-storage medium, they're capable of containing not only the audio data of the individual samples but also information regarding the original pitch of each sample (ie its *root key*) as well as any loop points it might contain. Unlike sample CDs, CD-ROMs can also contain ready-prepared multisamples that can be simply loaded into the sampler and played – provided, of course, that it's the right type of sampler. And there's the rub: different manufacturers tend to use different data formats, so a grand-piano sample designed for the samplers of Manufacturer X can't generally be read by those produced by Manufacturer Y; the data is managed differently because the two samplers have different internal structures. Some manufacturers even employ proprietary CD formats, making it impossible for their machines to recognise each other's disks.

The CD-ROMs discussed here are designed to be used with hardware samplers, but there are other formats, such as that used for CDs designed to be used with a computer. As a rule, these collections are structured in the same manner as audio CDs and generally don't contain ready-to-play multisamples. However, unlike audio CDs, their data is already in a computer-compatible format, such as WAV or AIFF, which means that, instead of having to be imported and converted, they can be copied straight onto a computer's hard disk. In these formats, the loop points are generally integrated into the samples, which spares you the laborious task of creating them yourself.

A vast range of sample CDs and CD-ROMs can be obtained from major suppliers like Best Service (www.bestservice.de) in many different formats and for every conceivable application. However, CD-ROMs designed for specific samplers can often be very expensive, costing as much as £100 apiece, whereas those designed for desktop computers tend to be more reasonably priced.

Over the years, the sample format developed by Akai has become established as a universally recognised standard, since the firm established itself quickly in the market with a range of hardware samplers that proved immensely popular and the format soon became very widespread. Today, most hardware and software samplers support Akai format as well as the proprietary CD format used by Akai disks. When you load an Akai sample, not only the audio data but also parameters like the root-key assignment, loop points and filter, envelope and LFO settings should all ideally be adopted automatically.

In short, it probably makes sense to splash out on CD-ROMs that contain high-quality instrument sounds – ie carefully organised, looped samples that you can

shape and polish further using your own sampler – as preparing material like this yourself is likely to prove very time consuming, and most people are only too happy to pay to be relieved of the chore. However, there's little sense in forking out a lot of cash for a CD-ROM that contains just sound textures and effects assigned to different notes on the keyboard, or folders full of drum and synth loops, as this kind of material can be obtained much more cheaply via sample CDs and isn't particularly difficult to import and organise.

# Effects

There are many effects devices and software modules available today that you can use to shape and refine both acoustic and electronic sounds, as well as the overall sonic image. They can be used to apply processing either to the entire signal or to a copy of it, which can then be mixed with the original at a later stage in the signal chain. The subject of mixing and effects processing is looked at in some detail later in this book, but the following section gives a brief introduction to the subject and an overview of the various types of effect that are used most commonly.

### Dynamic Processors

Among the most important (and least obtrusive) types of effect are those used to alter just the frequency content and amplitude levels of audio signals. The two most common dynamic effects are compressors and expanders, which respectively compress and expand the audio material's dynamic range (ie the ratio of the loudest to the quietest part of the signal).

Compressors automatically turn down the volume whenever the signal exceeds a user-defined level. Suppose, for example, that you've recorded a vocal track where the quietest passages are just a little too quiet, but when you turn up the overall volume the loudest passages are then so loud that they distort. The solution here is to use a compressor, which will turn down the level of the loudest passages but leave the rest of the recording unchanged, thus reducing the contrast between the loudest and softest passages (ie the recording's dynamic range). This can be useful when you want to increase the overall (ie average) level of a recording without incurring distortion.

Of course, compression can be applied to a number of instruments, not just vocals. Today, it's virtually indispensable for drum sounds, giving them a stronger and more penetrating sound, while it's often also applied in varying doses to the final mix, increasing the overall impact of the recording.

Although compressors offer few parameters, it's important to understand the ones they do have. The Threshold parameter determines the level above which the audio is compressed. The Ratio parameter, meanwhile, determines how much compression is applied; if the ratio is 2, for example, for every 2dB the uncompressed signal exceeds the threshold, the compressed signal will exceed it by only 1dB, whereas if the ratio is set to –10dB or higher, the compressor effectively acts as a limiter, preventing the level from ever exceeding the threshold by more than a very small amount.

Two other parameters relate to the agility of the response: Attack, which determines how soon compression is applied when the signal strays above the threshold, and Release, which determines how soon the level returns to normal when the signal falls back beneath the threshold.

**Cubase SX's VST Dynamics plug-in brings several dynamic functions together in a single window**

Since adding compression effectively reduces a signal's overall level, a further Make-up Gain parameter is generally provided to compensate by increasing it.

The second most important dynamic processor, the expander, offers almost the same parameters as the compressor but works the other way around and usually on the quietest parts of the audio, rather than the louder parts. Basically, expanders increase the dynamic range of a signal, usually by making quiet signals still quieter (known as *downward expansion*), and they can be very useful devices. For example, if you've interviewed someone outside and you've picked up someone else's voice as well as theirs, or a bird singing in the background, by setting the Threshold parameter to a level lower than that of the principal speaker, but louder than that of the unwanted content, the gain (ie the amplification) is reduced when the interviewee stops talking. As soon as he starts again, the gain is restored to its original level.

So the compressor reduces the gain when the signal level goes *above* the threshold and the expander reduces it when the signal goes *below* the threshold. However, a more drastic form of expander is known as a *noise gate*, which, rather than reducing the gain when the signal falls below a certain level, eliminates the signal altogether. Noise gates are useful tools for eliminating the buzzing or other low-frequency noise that's sometimes present in electric-guitar signals yet only becomes obtrusive when the programme material falls silent, such as during pauses in a solo.

### Equalisers

Like compressors and expanders, equalisers aren't normally classed as effects devices, but this is still a good time to discuss them as they also play a crucial role in improving signal quality. They complete the triumvirate of fundamental tools used at the mixing stage, along with compressors and expanders.

While dynamic processors operate on the signal level, equalisers act on the frequency response – for example, by turning up the bass or treble, just like the tone controls on your hi-fi. However, while tone controls on domestic equipment generally apply equalisation very simply and in a uniform way, equalisers take a wide range of forms and offer a number of additional parameters.

The equalisers found in studio equipment are understandably more sophisticated than those on domestic equipment as they have a far more complex set of tasks to perform, one of which is essentially to prevent collisions between instruments that possess fundamentals or formants (ie characteristic overtones) that occupy similar portions of the frequency spectrum. In such cases, an equaliser will exaggerate the differences and downplay the similarities between the two instruments. The subject of equalisation will be covered in greater detail later in this book, but here's a brief look at the various types of equaliser that are commonly encountered.

The type of equaliser commonly found in domestic hi-fi systems is actually a shelving equaliser, which boosts or attenuates frequencies above (in the case of the Treble control) or below (in the case of the Bass control) certain frequencies. In most hi-fi amps, these two frequencies – the corner frequency of the Treble and Bass controls – are fixed, and turning the knob controls the gain (variable within a ±15dB range) of the signal's effected portions. In other words, frequencies above the Treble control's shelving frequency can be boosted or attenuated by as much as 15dB. With some shelving EQs, the corner frequencies of the Treble or Bass controls (or the 'Hi and Lo shelving filter', as they're labelled in pro recording equipment) are programmable.

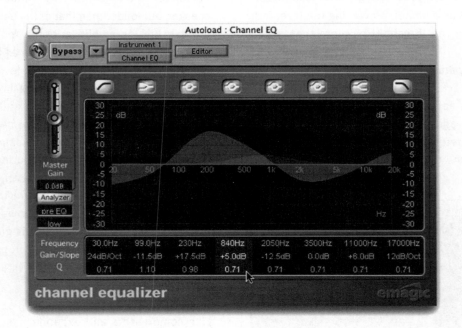

**Logic 6 Platinum's Channel Equalizer offers eight bands of EQ**

When it comes to correcting mid-range frequencies, things get a little more complicated. Here the equaliser acts on a band of frequencies that fall on either side of a central frequency, which is usually programmable (ie *sweepable*). Some equalisers even come equipped with a 'Q' control to determine the width of this band, in which case the equaliser is described as being 'fully parametric' or as offering 'variable Q'. Those that don't provide this facility are described as being 'semi-parametric' and as offering only 'constant Q'. Fully parametric equalisers are very flexible and allow precise intervention in the frequency response, which can be extremely useful when dealing with problematic signals.

Another type of equaliser often encountered in the home, though of limited value in the studio, is the graphic equaliser. Graphic EQs offer a row of sliders whose positions represent graphically the device's frequency response. Each slider controls the level of a set band of frequencies, and the more sliders there are, the closer together the central frequencies of these

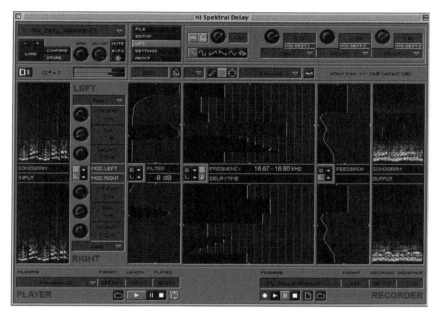

**FFT-based effects such as the NI Spektral Delay can affect signals in a particularly detailed and even drastic way**

bands. With 11-band equalisers, for example, the bands are distributed at one-octave intervals across the frequency spectrum, whereas with 31-band equalisers the distance between bands is a major third.

## Echo And Delay Effects

Echo is one of the classic effects, if not *the* classic effect, used in music production. Essentially, it involves mixing a delayed copy of the signal with the original in order to create a single echo. However, if the delay unit's output is fed back into its input, the result will be a series of echoes, each one fainter than the one that preceded it – provided, of course, that the gain applied to the feedback (or 'regeneration') signal has a value of less than 1.

Delay units are used to create atmosphere and the impression of space and depth, and so are used frequently and in many different ways in music production. If the length of the delay is synchronised to the tempo of the music, interesting rhythmic effects can be achieved.

Simple mono effects gave way long ago to elaborate delay units, including the *stereo delay*, which produces independent echoes for the left and right channels; the

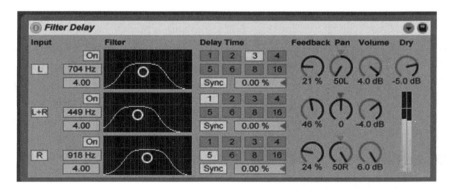

**The Filter Delay in Ableton Live offers three feedback paths, each with its own feedback filter – great for way-out dub effects**

*ping-pong delay*, which produces independent echoes for the left and right channels with their feedbacks crossed; and the *multi-tap delay*, which is the standard 'delay-plus-feedback' configuration but with the possibility of tapping the signal at multiple points along the delay line.

## Reverb

Reverberation is the second most important effect, and creating really good artificial reverb requires a great deal of skill. Good artificial reverb should sound dense, three-dimensional and natural rather than tinny, austere and clattery.

Natural reverb consists of multiple reflections of sound waves from the ceiling, floor, walls and objects within the room, and so the nature of the reverb depends on factors such as the size and shape of the room, the position of the sound source within it and the reflectivity of the surfaces of the room and its contents. For example, as the sound hits the ceiling, only some of the energy is reflected, the rest being absorbed. How much is absorbed and how much is reflected depends on the material from which the ceiling is constructed.

The onset of natural reverberation is gradual. If you clap your hands in a church, for example (and if you're going to try this, make sure there isn't a sermon being taken at the time!), you'll hear the direct sound and then nothing at first, as it takes a moment for the sound to travel to the nearest reflective surface and back. To imitate this, reverb effects insert a delay before the first reflections are produced.

The next thing you'll hear are the early reflections, a series of individual echoes whose timing depends

**Plug-ins like TC Works' Native Reverb Plus are equipped with displays that illustrate the reverb parameters**

on the geometry of the room and the position of the listener within it. These reflections represent the acoustic fingerprint of the room and are vital for obtaining an authentic and natural reverb. In fact, sometimes the term *reverberation* is defined sometimes to include and sometimes to exclude these early reflections, but this is just a matter of terminology.

Soon the reflections begin to arrive thick and fast. Instead of being perceptible only as distinct echoes and impossible to localise, late reflections are a result of the sound following ever more indirect paths to the listener, having bounced perhaps several times from the walls, floor and ceiling. This is known as the *diffuse reverberation*, which is thought to be the primary factor in establishing a sense of room size.

Gradually the sound field collapses and decays due to friction and the absorptivity of the reflective surfaces, whereby the higher frequencies are absorbed more rapidly than the lower ones, leading to a dulling of the sound as it dies away. The speed at which the energy field as a whole decays and at which the higher frequencies (in particular) are attenuated are therefore critical factors in obtaining a convincing reverb effect.

## Modulation Effects

Modulation effects are designed to add fullness and movement to the sound, and all operate by creating cyclic changes in a signal via an LFO. Typical modulation effects include chorus, flanger and phaser, all of which are based around delay effects but which sound very different from one another.

Chorus is used to make electric pianos or pads sound more lush, creating an impression of the signal being duplicated once or even many times and transforming the sound of a single vocalist to that of a choir. From a technical point of view, the effect is achieved by adding a delayed version of the signal to the original. The delay time (of between 10–40ms) isn't constant but is modulated by an LFO in order to achieve a shimmering effect as the speeding up and slowing down of the delayed signal causes the two signals to drift apart and then converge in tuning. Sometimes feedback is added, making the effect more pronounced. Chorus simulates the effect of two or more instruments or voices playing together, never perfectly in time nor perfectly in tune.

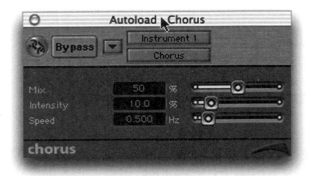

**Although it has few parameters, chorus is nevertheless a sophisticated effect**

**Cubase's Fuzzbox is designed to look like an effects pedal and simulates transistor distortion**

The flanger, meanwhile, is a close cousin of the chorus. It, too, is based on the idea of a modulated delay, although it's different in that the delay applied is much shorter (1–10ms) and the result is a cyclic discolouration of the signal, with the sound becoming increasingly metallic as more feedback is applied, creating a very striking effect reminiscent of a jet engine.

Finally, phasers employ frequency-dependent phase-shifting rather than signal delay (which is independent of frequency), but they produce results that are similar to (although not as pronounced as) flanging. Phasing was much used in the '70s, when it was applied discreetly sometimes to individual instruments and sometimes to an entire mix. The effect is created by sweeping a notch filter up and down through a given frequency range and summing the output with the original input.

## Distortion

Deliberately distorting a signal isn't a practice restricted to electric guitarists; it's also used often in computer-based music production. Distortion adds a little welcome grunge to the squeaky-clean digital universe, which is doubtless why it's so popular. Prime candidates for distortion are the bass, drums, synths and vocals.

As any guitarist will tell you, there are various types of distortion, each with a very different character. However, there is a fundamental distinction between valve (or tube) -based distortion, which is a comparatively benign and warm overdrive effect, and the far more aggressive fuzz of transistor-based

distortion. Within each category, there are further distinctions, with different manufacturers favouring different sounds.

Computer-based music production also makes use of additional forms of distortion, derived from the related worlds of synthesisers and digital technology. For instance, *wave shaping* and *wave wrapping* involve the manipulation of a signal through the application of various rules, such as horizontal reflection, leading to the creation of new overtones and new forms of distortion.

Another very popular technique for introducing distortion and grunge to a sound is by artificially degrading the digital audio resolution by reducing the word length and sampling frequency – ie those parameters that constitute the yardstick by which the quality of digital audio is assessed. These effects can be used independently or in combination. A shortening of the word length leads to a harshening of the sound, adding both distortion and graininess, while reducing the sampling frequency simultaneously reduces and distorts the high-frequency content of the signal. A massive reduction of the sampling frequency results in the signal becoming increasingly unrecognisable and overlaid with noise.

## Other Effects

As well as the effects described so far, there are one or two others that have proved their worth many times over in music production and deserve to be considered as part of the standard package. These include pitch-manipulating effects and so-called harmonisers or pitch shifters. (The terms *pitch shifter* and *harmoniser* describe the same effect, although the word 'Harmonizer' is a registered trademark owned by manufacturer Eventide.)

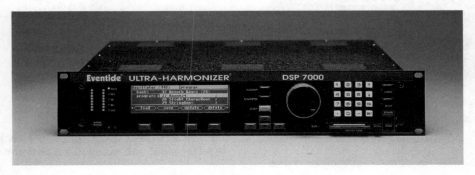

**Elegant and useful but not cheap, Eventide's Harmonizer DSP7000 proves that hardware can be beautiful**

Pitch shifters make it possible to double a guitar or vocal part a fifth or octave above the original pitch, or even to transpose it. Many pitch shifters also offer scale-correction facilities so that the transposition produces only notes that belong to the current scale. It's then possible to apply a kind of tonal quantising, whereby any note sung slightly out of tune snaps to the nearest scale tone.

Other effects, such as the Exciter™ and enhancer, are designed to improve the sound of individual signals – or, indeed, an entire mix – by adding high-frequency components to the signal to make it brighter and more transparent. Similarly, beefing up the sub-bass region can add punch or ballast to a mix. The attack and decay transients of sounds can also be manipulated in various ways in order to be made softer or crisper.

One other useful device that can be thought of as an effect is the vocoder. This device makes it possible to take a *carrier* signal (such as a melody played on the synth) and assign to it the sonic characteristics of a second signal, known as the *modulator*. If, for example, the modulator signal was a recording of someone talking, the result would be a talking synth. The vocoder achieves this by dividing both signals into a number of different frequency bands and then assigning the level of each band in the modulator signal to the corresponding band in the carrier, so that the carrier contains only those frequencies that are present in the modulator signal and takes on its sonic characteristics.

In a book like this, it's impossible to provide an exhaustive, or even a systematic, look at the many effects currently available, since a great deal of imagination often goes into creating new effects, making them hard to categorise. Not only that but new special effects, varieties of effect and

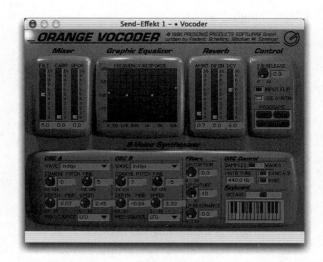

**Prosoniq's Orange Vocoder offers an integrated eight-voice synth as a carrier signal**

combinations of effects are being released on a more or less daily basis.

This is another part of modern music that's subject to the whims and vagaries of fashion. A new effect used imaginatively in one recording is likely to inspire a host of imitators until the effect becomes overused and familiar. At this point, some newer effect takes its place on the cutting edge until it, too, becomes old news. Of course, there are some effects once spurned by musicians that have enjoyed a brief revival, but most live for a brief instant and then vanish from popular culture for good.

## Latency

Latency is a phenomenon that was once – and, in some cases, still is – the prime bugbear of computer-based music-making. Fortunately, it's a problem that has been largely solved for users of Mac OS X, which is a state-of-the-art operating system specially tailored for the processing of audio and video data, but it's nonetheless important to understand what latency is and how to deal with it.

Latency is defined as the sum of the delays that arise from the processing of audio signals in the computer. The problem is that your computer has other things to do than simply processing and outputting audio; it also has to control the user interface, draw and redraw the screen, manage network connections, etc, all of which is a drain on the available processor resources. In order to stop the audio data stream from being interrupted while the CPU attends to these vital matters, it's buffered in various places. However, while this might solve the problem of continuity, it also inserts a delay into the system, the extent of which is directly proportional to the size of the buffers.

This can pose serious problems in practice. Suppose, for example, that you've loaded a software instrument and connected a MIDI keyboard to your computer. Now suppose that each time you press a key, half a second elapses before the note is heard. Half a second might not sound much, but it's enough to render the instrument all but unplayable.

This type of latency is known as *MIDI–Audio latency*. Here, the MIDI messages from the keyboard are received by the computer and passed on almost

immediately to the tone generator, which acts on the (at this stage, almost latency-free) messages, creating the sound, and then sends it to the computer's operating system or audio driver so that it can be output by its audio hardware. It's here that the signal is buffered and consequently delayed. In this case, therefore, the latency originates on the output side.

However, there are other forms of latency. Suppose you were recording your own rhythm-guitar track, monitoring your performance over headphones linked to the computer. Here, the guitar signal is fed into the computer's audio input, where it's buffered once and then returned to the audio output, where it's buffered a second time. In this case, there are two sources of latency, the input and output buffers, and the latency is cumulative with the result being that, when you strum a chord, it can take as long as a second before you hear the sound in the headphones, making it difficult, if not impossible, to lay down the guitar track.

Latencies as high as a second, or even half a second, are plainly intolerable from the standpoint of the performer, but these are the kinds of latencies that were produced by outdated, cheap PC sound cards with MME drivers, which were never intended for serious music-making in the first place. Thankfully, these sound cards have now largely been superseded.

With the various audio solutions for Mac (OS 9 or earlier) or PC, the degree of latency is a function of the quality of the audio driver, and it can vary from 20–40ms at worst to 5–20ms at best. The best audio solutions and drivers are even capable of reducing latency to 5ms or less, although this is achieved partly through the use of small buffers, which in turn impose a considerable drain on the CPU.

As is so often the case, the problem of latency is best approached pragmatically. While it's always best to get as low a latency as possible, you don't need to sacrifice too much to achieve this. Any argument about whether or not latency of a few milliseconds is bearable is rendered redundant when you consider that a drummer sitting a metre away from his monitors will be receiving the signal around 3ms after it has been sent, simply because that's how long it takes for the sound to travel one metre. If the monitors are three metres away, the latency will be around 10ms, and drummers play live under these kinds of conditions all the time.

The good news is that Mac OS X users can largely forget about the problem of latency. Even using the built-in audio hardware, the current generation of Macs can achieve latencies as low as 10ms without imposing any significant strain on the processor, so it's hard to see how latency could pose a problem.

# 2  THE MAC

This chapter looks at the hardware of the modern Macintosh and examines the suitability of the various types of Mac – both desktop and laptop models – for music applications.

As well as a look at the most modern Macs, there's also a breakdown of their immediate predecessors – the devices, in other words, upon with Mac OS X can sensibly run. It's true that Apple claims that its new operating system will run on all the older G3 computers (even the very first G3 Power Book), but Mac OS X pretty much exhausts the capabilities of some of them, leaving very little processing power over for the complexities of working with audio software, and processor upgrades aren't supported by Mac OS X, according to Apple.

## Which Mac Can Do What?

If you're planning on working in different locations or playing live, Power Books and iBooks obviously score over desktop models as they are easily portable. However, there are other differences between the various models that are less obvious but still need to be taken into consideration.

### Audio Inputs And Outputs

In the simplest case, you'll be wanting to use your computer straight out of the box, using nothing more than the integrated audio hardware. Every Mac is equipped with audio outputs, but not all offer audio inputs. Of course, whether or not you'll be happy with the inputs supplied is likely to depend on your requirements and how demanding you are when it comes to audio quality.

At the time of writing, with the exception of the G5, Apple computers integrate only analogue audio connections. Their output sockets are typical Walkman-style mini jacks, so if you want to connect your machine up to a stereo system, you'll need a cable with a stereo mini jack at one end and two normal RCA connectors at the other. You should be able to find one at your local music shop or any outlet supplying electronics equipment or computer accessories. If you don't connect the output to an amp or stereo system, you'll be stuck with listening to your material over the built-in loudspeakers, which are obviously inadequate for the requirements of music production.

Meanwhile, the audio input – if your machine has one – is also connected via a mini-jack socket. With the right lead, you can input both microphone and line signals at this port.

### Processing Power

Audio processing – which includes tone generation, mixing, applying effects in real time, etc – is a highly processor-intensive task made possible only by the rapid increase in the speed of computers in recent years. Only video editing imposes greater demands on the performance of modern computers.

Unlike writing emails, for instance, when you're making music with modern applications, it's easy to reach the limit of the computer's capabilities – and often a lot faster than you might have wished. Of course, how quickly this happens depends on your way of working, but it also depends on the overall power of your computer, and here there are several factors at work.

The most important factor is the power of the CPU. Currently, the Macs that Apple recommends as being suitable for OS X are supplied with G4 or G5 processors running at speeds from 1–2.5GHz. Of course, it's impossible to say here which system is the best for your individual requirements, but you'd nevertheless be advised to get a computer with at least a 400MHz G3 processor or, better still, a G4 or G5. The G4 processor, with its AltiVec 128-bit vector architecture – which allows the simultaneous parallel processing of many data items – is 10% faster than a G3 running at the same clock rate, even when running applications that aren't specially adapted for it. And if you're running programs that *are* designed to make use of the AltiVec unit, the difference could be as great as 30% or more. If you're going to be using audio applications, however, what's of crucial importance is how fast the computer is at performing floating-point arithmetic.

## The Hard Disk

The second most important aspect of performance is the computer's hard disk. When you're working on a project involving a large number of audio tracks with long audio files, the Mac has to be able to read all this data from the hard disk quickly. Short snippets of audio are generally read from RAM, but with longer files music applications will be constantly accessing the hard disk.

As with virtually all computer components, the last few years have seen standards of hard-disk performance come on in leaps and bounds, and modern hard disks are capable of playing back well over 100 audio tracks simultaneously, while with older computers – Power Books in particular – the hard disk could sometimes limit the number of tracks you were able to play back. Even so, the smaller hard disks of modern laptops are generally slower than the larger disks used by desktop computers.

Besides its speed, the size of the disk – or, rather, the amount of free space on it – is of crucial importance. It's a great luxury not to have to worry about hard-disk capacity – and this should certainly be the case with the new G5 and G4 models, which support hard-disk capacities as high as 500GB and 720GB respectively – but the size of disk you'll need will depend on both the task in hand and how you actually go about doing it.

Remember that one minute of CD-quality stereo in AIFF or WAV format will consume around 10MB of your hard disk, so an entire audio CD will take up around 700MB. A typical three-and-a-half-minute song, recorded on 12 stereo tracks in CD quality, will consequently require around 420MB of hard-disk space.

## CD And DVD Writers

Since audio data takes up a tremendous amount of space and hard disks can quickly become full, you'll need an efficient system for storing and archiving data – something like a CD writer, for example, which will enable you not only to record your music onto an audio CD that any CD player can read but also to create a copy of all the data of each completed project, in case you should ever wish to resume work on it.

Currently, some models of Mac – such as the eMac, the most affordable version – offer a Combo drive, which allows you to read DVDs and read and write CDs, while the more expensive models are equipped with what Apple calls a SuperDrive, which allows you to read and write both CDs and DVDs that will play in almost any standard DVD player. The SuperDrive burns DVDs at 4x playback speed (8x on the G5).

Used as a normal data-storage medium, a DVD-R is capable of storing 4.7GB of data, whereas a normal CD-R can handle a maximum of only 700MB. If you're working on long audio projects, a DVD writer is a great solution for backing up and archiving, but the most important thing is to make sure you have either a DVD writer or a CD writer.

## RAM

Whereas the speed of the computer's processor might represent the system's horsepower, the RAM (Read-Only Memory) is the equivalent of cubic capacity, and it's a commonly held belief that you can never have too much RAM. Up to a point, this is true; according to the instruction leaflet that comes with Mac OS X, your machine must have at least 128MB of RAM, but for music applications you really do need more.

Mac OS X provides a lavish graphic interface, but the effects that it employs, such as transparency, take up a considerable amount of RAM. Remember that, when RAM is in short supply, the operating system stores data temporarily on the hard disk, causing the system's performance to become sluggish, since accessing the hard disk is considerably slower than accessing RAM, particularly when the computer is trying to play back multiple audio tracks at the same time.

If a computer has plenty of RAM, the operating system has somewhere to store the bits and bobs in needs in order to function smoothly that it can access far more rapidly than the hard disk. For music applications, therefore, you want at least 256MB and, if possible, 384MB or more of RAM. The more powerful models now employ a new high-speed type of memory known as PC3200 DDR (Double Data Rate) SDRAM, which operates at 400MHz for up to 6.4GBps (gigabytes per second) throughput.

Another aid to performance is the L3 cache, which uses up to 2MB of high-speed DDR SRAM and boosts the processor's performance by providing lightning-fast access to data and application code at up to 4GBps.

## Buss Speed

The processor's buss speed indicates the speed at which data travels inside the computer. On older Macs, the buss speed was 66MHz, which was later increased to 100MHz, and the current G4 desktops now offer buss speeds of 133MHz and 167MHz. The fastest data access of all, and by a massive margin, is offered by the Power Mac G5, in which each of the two processors has its own front-side buss running at half the speed of the processor, which means that the front-side busses of the G5 run at 900MHz, 1GHz or 1.25GHz, depending on the model (the portable Macs lag behind the desktop models in this respect.) However, while being an indicator of the power of the entire system, the buss speed isn't as important a factor as the speed of the processor. All things being equal, of course, you should still choose the model with the faster buss speed.

## PCI Slots

For a long time, PCI cards were the method of choice when it came to expanding or upgrading the functionality of a desktop Mac and were used for integrating things like optional audio hardware. Nowadays, while PCI cards are still available, even for Mac OS X, their importance is on the wane, as made evident by the recent success of the iMac and the current crop of laptops, none of which are equipped to accept PCI cards.

Today, the importance of PCI slots has been undermined by the advent of the USB and FireWire interfaces, which allow you to integrate most peripherals into your system via cable or even via radio. Devices connected via the USB or FireWire ports can also be used with laptops, whereas PCI cards can't (at least, not without being prohibitively expensive).

The Power Mac G5 models with 2.0GHz and 2.5GHz dual processors come with three PCI-X slots. The PCI-X protocol supports high-performance PCI devices, increasing speeds dramatically from 33MHz to 133MHz and throughput from 266MBps to 2GBps.

## PC Card Slots

PC cards – once known as *PCMCIA cards* – are used by Power Books and PC laptops as well as (occasionally) by handheld computers.

A large number of peripherals are available in PC-card format, from modems and a number of different interfaces to mini hard disks and even audio interfaces. However, the choice of available devices is comparatively small and most are very expensive, so you shouldn't regard a PC card slot as an indispensable feature for music production. Here, too, USB and FireWire solutions are at a competitive advantage as they can be used with both desktops and laptops, whereas desktop computers generally don't offer PC card slots.

## USB

Since the days of the first iMacs, all Macintoshes have been equipped with at least one USB (Universal Serial Buss) port which can be used to connect a mouse, a scanner, floppy and CD-ROM drives, webcams and all kinds of other accessories to the computer. When it comes to music production, the USB interface is used primarily for connecting MIDI interfaces, copy-protection dongles and optional audio hardware. It is therefore very useful (although not essential) to have at least one USB port. Older computers, such as the Wall Street series of Power Books, can be upgraded with USB connectors via PC card and desktops via PCI, and if you don't have enough USB ports for a particular application, you can increase the number of ports available with a USB hub. In theory, you can connect over 100 devices to a single USB port through the use of hubs.

## FireWire

Originally co-developed by Apple, the FireWire interface (also known as IEEE 1394 and Sony iLink) has been a feature of all Macs for some time now. Running at 400MBps (or 800MBps with the new standard), the current generation of FireWire interfaces are becoming increasingly popular and are widely used particularly in the video sector; in fact, virtually all modern DV cameras are equipped with one of these interfaces, allowing films to be transferred quickly and easily to the computer for editing.

The FireWire interface is also gaining ground in the music sector for use with optional (and usually multichannel) audio interfaces. It offers a bandwidth many times wider than the rather sluggish USB 1 standard, and using it to transfer multiple audio signals imposes considerably less of a burden on the computer than transferring the same amount of data via USB would. The development of USB 2 did close the gap somewhat, but with the release of the new IEEE 1394b standard, with its 800MBps throughput, FireWire again has the edge. As with USB, FireWire ports can be supplied by both PCI and PC cards.

Any manufacturer can develop and use the FireWire procedures and protocols for the connection of its audio interfaces, although it appears that the mLAN protocol developed by Yamaha is currently emerging as the most widely recognised protocol for transmitting audio and MIDI data via FireWire. Around 100 companies have already united to form an interest group with a view to producing gear that is fully cross-compatible with the mLAN protocol.

## Displays

When it comes to music production, you're best off having a screen with a resolution of at least 1024 x 768 pixels. If your screen is capable of even higher resolution, so much the better, but if you have a monitor that's capable of only 800 x 600 screen resolution, you're going to be struggling because the user interfaces of most music applications take up a

great deal of space on the screen, and having to scroll constantly can become very tiresome.

The actual physical size of the screen is less important than how much detail can be displayed on it at once (unless, of course, your eyesight's not the best). Most of the latest crop of laptops from Apple have screen resolutions of 1024 x 768 or better, whereas with the first generation of iBooks it was only 800 x 600 pixels.

At the top end of the range, Apple's new widescreen Cinema Displays for the Power Mac G5, the G4 and the Power Book G4 include models with 20", 23" and 30" high-definition displays (currently priced at £999, £1,549 and £2,549, respectively), the latter of these offering a staggering 4 million pixels, which would allow you to display 126 Logic mixer controls simultaneously! Each display is designed to match the sculpted aluminium enclosures of the Power Mac G5 and Power Book and is mounted on an elegant curved stand, with the viewing angle easily adjustable from –5° to 25°, while the DVI connection even allows you to use the same screen for your PC, if you have one. The 30" Cinema HD Display (for the G5 only and currently retailing at £450) is actually so big that it requires a special graphics card, the NVIDIA GeForce 6800 Ultra DDL, which delivers 2,560 x 1,600 resolution and the capacity to drive two 30" displays side by side.

## Wireless Connectivity

If there's no telephone point available in the room, stage or studio where you've set up your Mac, it's possible to connect to the Internet at 54MBps by inserting an AirPort Extreme Card, which is capable of communicating with an AirPort Extreme Base Station (connected to the phone jack) up to 150 feet away. Most models of Macintosh – including all Power Books – also offer Bluetooth technology, which connects wirelessly to digital devices, including Bluetooth-enabled mobile phones, handhelds and peripherals. You can also use it to synchronise personal information between your computer, your mobile phone and your Palm OS-based handheld. Also, if your laptop is Bluetooth-compatible, you can use any Bluetooth-enabled mobile phone to take advantage of GPRS or 1xRTT connectivity, allowing you to check your email from just about anywhere.

## The Current Models

Now you've got an idea of what features to look for and their relative importance when it comes to music production, here's a quick guide to the current crop of Macs on the market, just in case you haven't yet bought one and you need a little guidance.

### Power Mac G5

The new Power Mac G5 series comprises three models, each employing dual G5 processors running at speeds of either 1.8GHz, 2GHz or 2.5GHz. Mac OS X allows the G5 to divide up tasks between the two processors, whose 64-bit, high-bandwidth architecture makes these the fastest Macs ever produced.

Among the features that will be of most interest to musicians are the digital, optical and analogue ports that support both new and legacy hardware. In fact, the G5 is the first Mac to offer optical S/PDIF connectivity.

The standard system configurations offer 256MB or 512MB of high-speed 400MHz DDR SDRAM, but this

COURTESY OF APPLE

**Less noise, more power – the G5 desktops are the new dream machines in the Apple range**

memory is scalable up to 8GB, so the Power Mac G5 supports more audio tracks and plug-ins than any previous Power Mac and three times more than the G4. Also, fan noise – the perennial problem of the G4 models – has been reduced by 50% due to a new cooling system whereby the enclosure houses four discrete thermal zones to compartmentalise the primary heat-producing components, each of which boasts its own dedicated low-speed fan. Meanwhile, a sophisticated liquid cooling system governed by the operating system controls dynamically the flow of the fluid and the speed of the fans in response to changes in temperature.

The G5 models come with three 133MHz PCI-X slots, which offer throughput of 2GBps for high performance DSP hardware solutions. A removable side door gives you access to the slots and bays, enabling you to add more memory, a second hard drive or an AirPort Extreme card quickly and easily, without having to get out the toolbox. There are two Serial ATA hard drive bays for up to 500GB of fast internal data storage, and if you want more you can use a Fibre Channel PCI card to connect to Xserve RAID, Apple's high-performance storage system. All Power Mac G5 models offer a SuperDrive (DVD-R/CD-RW) capable of writing DVDs at 8x playback speed.

Power Mac G5 systems have a FireWire 400 port on the front and another on the back, as well as a FireWire 800 port on the back for high-bandwidth devices such as DV cameras, hard drives and digital music players. They also have two USB 1.1 ports on the keyboard and three USB 2.0 ports – one on the front and two on the back – for connecting keyboards, microphones and speakers as well as standard peripherals such as printers and scanners.

At the time of writing, the Power Mac G5 models are priced at £1,449 (1.8GHz), £1,849 (2GHz) and £2,199 (2.5GHz).

### Power Mac G4

Until recently the flagship of Apple desktops, the Power Mac G4 is designed for creative as well as business environments and can be custom-built to fit any professional use. Depending on your needs, you could opt for 2GB of high-speed DDR SDRAM, a 4x SuperDrive and up to four internal hard disk drives, which would give you a staggering 720GB of storage for your songs or projects. The G4 comes in both 1.25GHz single-processor and dual-processor configurations.

The Power Mac G4's system architecture offers a level of memory called an *L3 cache*, enabling it to access data much faster than from the hard disk or even from main memory. The L3 cache uses up to 2MB of high-speed DDR SDRAM, which boosts the processor's functionality by providing access to data and application code at up to 4GBps.

The Power Mac G4 is equipped with analogue inputs and outputs in mini-jack format, while current models also sport four full-length 64-bit, 33MHz PCI slots. These can be used in many ways to expand the functionality of your desktop, one of the most interesting (from the standpoint of music production) being the ability to output multichannel sound. FireWire, PCI expansion and Gigabit Ethernet are integrated directly into the main system controller, reducing latency and providing superior I/O performance.

However, PCI cards don't represent the only multi-channel solution; the four USB and two FireWire 400 ports (which are also offered by portable Macs) can also be used for multichannel applications, so while they're undoubtedly a plus, the PCI card slots can't be considered a conclusive argument in favour of the Power Mac G4. Processors can often be upgraded, so if you can live without dual processors for the time being, you might find a more affordable solution to your requirements elsewhere in the Mac range.

The G4 can be used with any of three displays – the 17" Apple Studio Display, the 20" Apple Cinema Display and the 23" Apple Cinema HD Display – and a choice of two graphics cards: the ATI Radeon 9000 Pro and the NVIDIA GeForce4 Titanium.

You should also be aware that many of the Power Mac G4 models are rather noisy, since they often have several fans in their cooling mechanisms, and not the quietest fans at that. This can be especially annoying when you're trying to compose, so unless you can afford a G5, you'll have to judge for yourself whether the G4's undoubted advantages over a laptop, in terms of processing power and expandability, are worth it in the light of this shortcoming.

Power Mac G4 models currently retail at £999 (1.25GHz), £1,219 (dual 1.25GHz) and £1,349 (dual 1.25GHz SuperDrive).

## iMac G4

Referred to affectionately as the 'table lamp', the iMac G4, with its swivelling display, seems to have been conceived more as an *objet d'art* for the home than for professional use. On this machine, things like PCI slots are dispensed with, the USB and FireWire interfaces being elegantly integrated into the hemispherical base. Nonetheless, in terms of performance, the iMac G4 is a perfectly credible alternative to the more conventionally styled models in the range and more than adequate for the needs of music production.

The iMac comes with a choice of three displays – a 20" widescreen (1,680 x 1,050 pixels), a 17" widescreen (1,440 x 900 pixels) and a 15" flat-panel display (1,024 x 768 pixels) – whose height and angle can be adjusted with just a touch. With 1.7 million pixels, the 20" display is obviously ideal for working with notation and sequencing software, although even the 15" screen is perfectly adequate for this purpose.

COURTESY OF APPLE

**Power Mac G4**

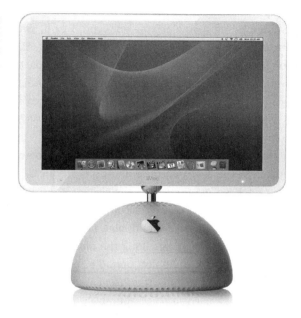

*Courtesy of Apple*

**The iMac: pretty but far from dumb**

All 20" and 17" iMacs are equipped with a 1.25GHz PowerPC G4 processor with Velocity Engine, 256MB of PC2700 (333MHz) Double Data Rate SDRAM main memory (expandable to 1GB), a SuperDrive, NVIDIA GeForce FX 5200 Ultra graphics card with 64MB of DDR SDRAM, and an Ultra-ATA/100 80GB hard disk running at 7,200rpm. The 15" model, meanwhile, has a slightly slower processor (1GHz PowerPC G4), a Combo drive (DVD-ROM/CD-RW) in place of the SuperDrive and NVIDIA GeForce4 MX graphics equipped with 32MB of DDR SDRAM, but is otherwise similarly equipped.

All models of iMac G4 offer built-in 10/100BASE-T Ethernet and 56k V.92 internal modem, two FireWire 400 ports, three USB 2.0 ports, two USB 1.1 ports (on the keyboard), a VGA output port, S-Video and composite video output, a headphone jack, Apple's speaker mini jack and an audio line-in jack. Given the generous provision of USB and FireWire ports, you don't have to rely upon the integrated audio inputs and outputs, and with the optional AirPort Extreme card, you can connect to the Internet at distances up to 50 metres from the nearest telephone jack.

At the time of writing, Apple has stopped taking orders for the current iMac in preparation for the launch of an all-new iMac line in September 2004. The prices are listed as £999 (15" combo), £1,449 (17" SuperDrive) and £1,749 (20" SuperDrive).

## eMac

Whether the E stands for *education* or *economy*, the eMac is certainly the most affordable model in the Mac range and the last to feature a screen with a cathode ray tube. This doesn't mean that it's unsuitable for music production, of course; after all, it's powered by the same G4 processor as the iMac, and its 17" flat 1,280 x 960-pixel CRT display is perfectly adequate for running sequencing software and large onscreen mixing displays. The machine comes bundled with a suite of iLife '04 applications, comprising iTunes, iPhoto, iMovie, iDVD and GarageBand.

*Courtesy of Apple*

**The eMac: just plug it in and switch it on**

The eMac comes with both an audio input and an audio output on mini jacks. The two lowest priced models come with CD writers and the larger model has a SuperDrive CD/DVD burner.

At the time of writing, the eMac is listed at £549 (Combo) and £699 (SuperDrive) including VAT.

## Power Book G4

No one has anything bad to say about Apple's Power Book range, which currently boasts five models: a 17" with SuperDrive and 15" and 12" models, each with either Combo or SuperDrive. With their large, high-resolution displays, the two larger models are almost as easy to work with as desktop models. And if you need an even bigger screen, the Power Book G4 offers a DVI port via which you can connect either the 20" Cinema Display or the 23" Cinema HD Display. Due to their large display sizes, these Power Books aren't especially small, but they're very light (2kg, 2.6kg and 3.1kg respectively) and flat, and are therefore highly portable.

The 12" models are about the same size as the white iBook and have the same screen resolution of 1,024 x 768 pixels, while the 15" models support resolutions up to 1,280 x 854 and the 17" up to 1,440 x 900 pixels. The three less expensive models of Power Book are driven by G4 processors with a Velocity Engine running at 1.33GHz, while the 15" and 17" run on G4 processors running at 1.5GHz and both have SuperDrives. The 1.33GHz models offer 256MB of PC2700 (333MHz) DDR SDRAM and 60GB hard disks, while the 1.5GHz models offer 512MB and 80GB, respectively, and so even the smallest models have easily enough processing power, memory and hard-disk space for music production. In fact, the larger models are ideal laptops for this kind of application.

All Power Books come with headphone output and a line-in socket, both of which take mini jacks, while

the 15" and 17" models also offer a PC card/CardBus slot supporting a single Type I or Type II card, which can be used for high-quality audio interfaces. Even though the 12" models don't include such a slot, this shouldn't be regarded as too much of a handicap because the USB 2.0 and FireWire 400 interfaces can be used for the same purpose. All models offer AirPort Extreme and Bluetooth as standard.

Most people who work with them quickly come to appreciate the fact that, like all Apple products, the Power Book is a masterpiece of engineering and software design. Of course, this isn't a conclusive argument in its favour, from a musical standpoint, but it's true to say that not only is the Power Book the most elegant but it's also the fastest of Apple's portable computers.

At the time of writing, the Power Book G4 models are listed at £1,149 (12" Combo), £1,299 (12" SuperDrive), £1399 (15" Combo), £1749 (15" SuperDrive) and £1,949 (17" SuperDrive).

## iBook G4

The iBook series contains the most affordable G4 notebooks in the Apple range. They come with either a 1GHz or a 1.2GHz PowerPC G4 processor with Velocity Engine and 512K of Level 2 cache, while the system buss runs at 133MHz, and with 256MB of RAM (expandable to a massive 1.25GB) there's plenty of onboard memory for running plug-ins. The hard drive capacity is 30GB for the model with a 12" screen, while the 14" models have either a 1GHz or 1.2GHz processor and either 40MB or 60MB, respectively. With extra-long-life batteries lasting up to six hours and lightweight but robust plastic cases, these machines are clearly designed with portability in mind; in fact, the lightest model in the series weighs just 2.2kg and comes with a 12.1" screen, but at 2.7kg the 14.1" model is scarcely much heavier and – according to Apple – fits snugly into a backpack. The display resolution for both models is 1,024 x 768 pixels.

iBooks are designed for home use – surfing the Internet, sending emails, doing homework, playing games, listening to CDs and watching DVD – but they're also ideal for music production in the home or on the road. The 1.25GHz model comes equipped with a built-in AirPort Extreme card, allowing you to connect to the

COURTESY OF APPLE

**Power Book G4**

**The iBook: robust, versatile and good value for money**

Internet up to 150 feet away from the nearest phone point, while all models feature a FireWire 400 and two USB 2.0 ports for connecting audio and MIDI hardware and standard peripherals, as well as a built-in 10/100BASE-T Ethernet connector. The iBook G4 comes as standard with a Combo drive, although you can order a SuperDrive for the 14" model, if you prefer.

At the time of writing, the iBook G4 models are priced at £799 (12"), £899 (14", 1GHz) and £1,049 (14", 1.2GHz).

## Older Macs

Mac OS X is supported by all G4 computers as well as all original G3 computers, with the exception of the very first G3 Power Book. However, many of the older computers – particularly those less well endowed with RAM – are likely to be pushed to their limits just running the operating system, and while your Internet browser, email client, graphics programs and word processor might function flawlessly in OS X, processor-intensive software like most current audio sequencers will quickly cause the system to run out of steam. This doesn't mean you won't be able to use them at all for music in OS X, only that you'll have to live within your means. With this in mind, here's a quick look at some older models of Macintosh whose special features might still prove useful.

### iBook G3

The iBook G3 was originally designed to be a consumer computer rather than one used professionally. In place of the robust and elegant metal of the Power Book, the iBook G3 came in a plastic case with the rucksack rather than the briefcase in mind. With only a G3 processor, it's a little slower than the current models, lacking also the G4's AltiVec Velocity Engine, but it's still perfectly adequate for music production.

The iBook G3 was robust and useful for making music as well as representing good value for money.

### iBook I

Likened to ladies' handbags by some and toilet seats by others, the models in the first iBook series aren't particularly well suited to music production. They're hampered by the moderate speed of their G3 processors, their 66MHz buss speed and the size of their displays, which at 800 x 600 pixel is too small for comfort when working with the latest music software. They also have no audio input and only the special graphite model offers a FireWire interface.

### iMac

The CRT iMacs suffer from much the same shortcomings as the iBook I models. The older machines are a little too slow and offer no FireWire port, and while these defects were remedied in the more recent models, these machines still suffer from the indifferent quality of their integrated screens. Even though these may offer a display resolution of 1024 x 768, the picture is somewhat blurred, which rather takes the joy out of working with them for long periods and can lead to eyestrain before long. Things look better at 800 x 600 resolution, but working this way involves a lot of tiresome scrolling.

### Power Book

Even though they might not be blindingly fast, the portability of the older G3 Power Books (Wall Street and Pismo models) makes them useful computers for working with onstage. Of the two models, the faster 300MHz Pismo generation has the edge.

With the G4 Power Book, you'd be advised to think twice about picking up a second-generation model (ie 500MHz and 667MHz machines) as the greater speed of their processors is said to be offset by a bottleneck in their memory-access system, and they're actually not much faster than the first-generation 400MHz and

500MHz models. And only by the time the third-generation 667MHz and 800MHz models hit the shelves did Apple include audio inputs; the earlier models offered only audio outputs.

## Power Mac G3/G4

Since the release of the original beige G3 Macs, many generations of G3 and G4 desktops have come and gone. Since the older G3s are capable of just 450MHz at best, if you're scouring the second-hand market you're best off holding out for a G4. And if you can find one with dual processors, so much the better as, unlike its various Classic predecessors, Mac OS X is automatically able to take advantage of the second processor.

Predictably, desktop models that were originally conceived as professional rather than consumer machines offer the best and most diverse expansion capabilities. All are equipped with PCI slots, which can be filled with audio-interface cards, and practically all can be upgraded with larger hard disks, CD/DVD writers, more RAM and even faster processors. You might even consider replacing the internal cooling fans with quieter models, as many Power Macs frankly make far too much noise.

# 3 THE SOFTWARE

Now that you have some idea of the fundamental principles behind modern Macintoshes and the hardware they use, it's time to consider the software they employ for making music. This chapter introduces the various types of application used in the production of music and gives a brief description of the best in each case.

Mac OS X is still a very new system, so there aren't yet as many applications available for it as there are for Mac Classic, although most of the market-leading programs have been released in OS X versions. Thankfully, the fog is also beginning to lift around the various interfaces offered by the system, and it's finally starting to become clear which interfaces are being supported by which software houses.

## Audio And MIDI Under Mac OS X
### Interfaces And Drivers

Music software on the Mac makes use of various interfaces and types of driver architecture for two fundamental purposes: to transfer audio data to and from the audio hardware or MIDI data to and from a connected MIDI device, and to allow different programs to work together, exchanging audio data and other information. Therefore, before diving into the various types of application that are available for music production, here's a quick look at this framework of interfaces and drivers.

### Core MIDI

Core MIDI is Mac OS X's own driver architecture for the management and use of MIDI devices. If you want to use an interface with MIDI inputs and outputs under Mac OS X, it must have a Core MIDI driver; there's no other

option. Once installed, the Core MIDI driver of a device is managed by the operating system and is therefore available to all programs. This management of MIDI devices and their drivers from a central location makes it possible for several applications to receive data from, and send data to, the same interface simultaneously.

If you want to see which Core MIDI drivers are installed on your system, simply double click the hard-disk icon in the Library → Audio → MIDI Drivers folder.

### Core Audio

Core Audio is the driver architecture for interfacing with audio hardware in Mac OS X, addressing the audio outputs and inputs (if present) supplied with your Mac and any optional hardware you might have installed. Usually, such hardware will be delivered with a Core Audio driver that has to be installed before the hardware can be used, although most hardware is already directly supported by Mac OS X and so no additional driver installation is required.

Since Core Audio drivers are also managed by the operating system, several programs can access the inputs and outputs of your audio hardware simultaneously, with the audio data streams of the programs managed by the driver where appropriate.

### ASIO

Under Mac OS 9 and Windows, ASIO drivers are often used for the integration of additional audio hardware. Originally developed by Steinberg, the ASIO driver architecture enables the use of multichannel audio hardware, as well as reducing latency.

Under Mac OS X, ASIO drivers aren't strictly necessary, since with Core Audio the operating system already offers a driver architecture suitable for professional music production. Even so, Steinberg software also supports ASIO under Mac OS X, which means that there are now two competing standards. Since Core Audio is Apple's own solution, it ought logically to be the one best adapted to Mac OS X, so unless both survive, it should be the one that prevails.

### Audio Units

The most important software applications for music production are generally designed to integrate software modules (often designed by third parties) that take care of special functions or extend the capabilities of the program in other ways. Such modules are known as *plug-ins*, and they might take the form of instruments or effects designed to be integrated into larger programs.

Here, too, standards are necessary to ensure that the software of different suppliers works together flawlessly, and for this reason Apple has developed a new plug-in interface for Mac OS X called Audio Unit. This interface allows compatible plug-ins to be installed at the system level, making them available to all applications that support the standard.

Apple's plug-in architecture is both modern and flexible, but it must nonetheless contend with the disadvantages of being both new and confined to the Macintosh platform. Just like the Core Audio drivers for audio hardware, plug-ins designed to the Audio Units standard are unknown in the world of Windows, which means that any manufacturers intending to support them will have to do rather more than just tweak the Windows versions of their software. Nonetheless, the new Apple interface has already won the support of all the major plug-in suppliers.

### VST

As well as defending its ASIO driver architecture, Steinberg is also standing by its VST plug-in interface, perhaps because it's a cross-platform standard and well established under both Windows and Mac OS 9. It's also supported by many of the major music applications, and there are a multitude of VST effects and instrument plug-ins that can be ported easily from one platform to the other.

This means that, just as with Core Audio and ASIO, there are now two competing standards under Mac OS X: Audio Unit and VST. Of course, if both standards were supported by all the major applications, there would be no problem, but sadly this is not the case, as we shall see shortly.

### ReWire

The ReWire software interface was developed by the Swedish firm Propellerhead Software, developers of Reason. Rather than a plug-in architecture in any simple sense of the term, ReWire is designed to allow two otherwise independent programs to run in tandem.

The ReWire link allows up to 64 audio channels to be transmitted from a ReWire slave to a ReWire master, with both applications running in perfect sync. With this kind of setup, if you start one program, the other starts simultaneously, while if you repeat a passage in one application, the equivalent passage in the other will also be repeated. The audio output comes from the ReWire master, so the output of the ReWire slave is normally fed into the master computer's mixer application.

## System Settings For Audio

Since the release of Jaguar (Mac OS X version 10.2), the audio settings for the Mac operating system are located in two different places. One is the Sound panel of the System Preferences dialog, from which you can select an audio input, the audio output and an alert tone, as well as make a few basic adjustments.

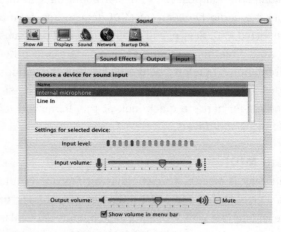

**The Input page of the Sound panel**

The available options for changing the audio input will depend on the model of Mac you're using, ranging from the integrated microphone of the Power Books to the mini-jack inputs offered by other models and any additional hardware you might have installed. Whichever model you're using, however, the level of the input signal should be set as high as possible to obtain the optimum audio resolution from the A/D converter without causing distortion.

**The Sound Effects page of the Sound panel contains functions allowing you to turn the user-interface effects down or off**

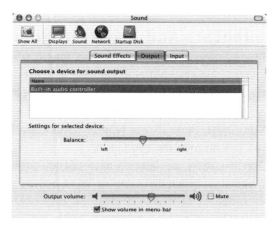

**The system-volume slider**

Under certain circumstances, it's also possible to choose from several different output options, although of course if your Mac is equipped with nothing more than the integrated audio output, this will be the only option displayed. The output volume can be set using the main volume slider, which can also be displayed in the Menu bar.

The first page of the Sound dialog box contains setting for alert noises, which are something like start-up noises and, as such, are anathema to anyone trying to make music on the Mac. Here you have the opportunity to turn down the volume of your alert noise or even assign it to a separate output. In fact, you're best off turning your alert noise down or even off entirely, along with all other sound effects, and activating visual effects via the Hearing page of the Universal Access panel in the System Preferences.

If you've connected the audio output to your hi-fi using a suitable lead (stereo mini jack at one end and dual RCAs at the other), you should ideally ensure that the computer's output level is about the same as

that of your CD player or cassette deck or whatever else you've connected to the hi-fi amp. This will save you having to rush to the amp in order to adjust the volume whenever you change from one sound source to another.

## The Audio MIDI Setup Utility

This little application is located in the Utilities sub-folder of the Applications folder. Essentially, it offers you the possibility of making more far-reaching adjustments to your computer's audio settings. The dialog box has two tabs, labelled 'Audio Devices' and 'MIDI Devices'.

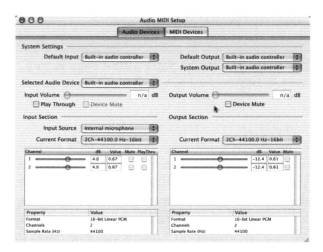

**The Audio MIDI Setup utility is used for setting the parameters of the hardware used with your system**

The top part of the Audio page contains options for selecting an input audio device, an output audio device and a device to provide the system sounds. If you're using only the integrated audio hardware, you'll just see the built-in audio controller, but if you have any other audio devices installed, they'll be available for selection here.

The various parameters in the lower part of the window relate to the device currently selected and include Level Adjustment from the Sound control field (for both stereo channels separately, if desired) and the number of channels and current audio format (sampling rate, word length, etc). These criteria can also be modified, as long as the audio hardware you're using permits this.

The MIDI page, meanwhile, allows you to manage your system's MIDI interface(s) – again, on a system-wide basis – and to establish MIDI connections.

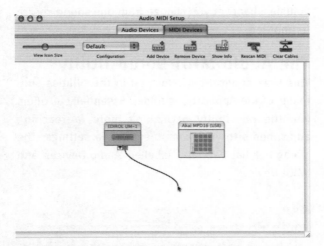

**The Audio MIDI Setup dialog's MIDI page can be used to connect up MIDI devices**

Normally there's nothing to do here, since after installation you activate a connected MIDI interface simply by selecting it within whatever audio program you're using. On rare occasions, however, the options displayed here can be useful; for example, if you have a device that receives only on channels 1–8, this information could be used by a certain application so that it doesn't show the device inappropriately in one of its drop-down or pop-up menus.

The previous illustration shows two installed MIDI devices, a MIDI interface and a pad controller, being used as an input instrument. Note that, by drawing cable connections here with the mouse, you're not creating software MIDI routings but simply providing MIDI applications with information about what devices are present. These options are mainly useful in conjunction with an extensive external MIDI system. Hopefully, in future versions of OS X, both pages in the Audio MIDI Setup dialog will be expanded.

## Sequencers And Major Programs

There are many aspects to making music with a computer – for example, you can use the Mac as a virtual instrument, as a substitute for a tape recorder or as an entire recording studio in one box. In every case, however, there is one type of application that plays a central role: the sequencer.

Over the years, sequencers have become steadily more versatile, gradually usurping the functions of a whole range of hardware devices once considered indispensable to music production. In the early days of modern computer-based music production – from the mid '80s to the early '90s – sequencers were used exclusively for controlling external synths and drum computers via MIDI.

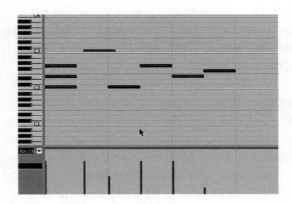

**A sequencer's piano-roll editor displaying MIDI notes in the top pane and key velocity in the bottom pane**

MIDI data was recorded by the computer, corrected, arranged, saved and later transmitted to external tone generators, which played back the right notes at the right time. Even the name *sequencer* harks back to the device's early days; in the synthesiser jargon of the time, a 'sequencer' was an independent device used to create short melodies with the help of a row of rotary controls.

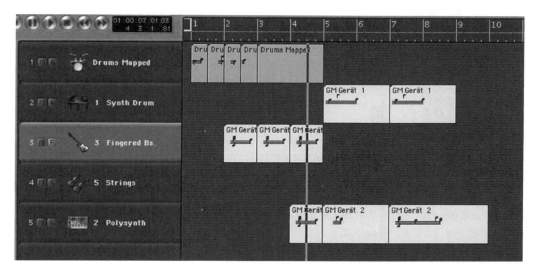

**MIDI data stored on sequencer tracks. The ruler at the top of the screen displays the bar and beat numbers, while the vertical line indicates the current song position**

Sequencers still function according to a principle that has stood the test of time, whereby MIDI data is recorded (or entered in some other way) on a number of individual tracks that are stacked vertically beneath a ruler showing either the elapsed time (measured from the start of the song) or the position of the data in bars and beats. Each track is normally dedicated to a different instrument, or else to a different patch (ie sound) within the same instrument. If the material hasn't been recorded in a single continuous take, each track will look like a series of blocks that can be edited and manipulated in many ways – such as by cutting and pasting – in order to correct errors in the performance.

While the essential principle hasn't changed, sequencing applications have come a long way since those early days. For a start, they now come equipped with a selection of editors, each offering a different way of manipulating various aspects of the data with specific tools. Depending on which editor you have open at any one time, the notes could be displayed as horizontal slits in a piano-roll-type display, diamonds indicating

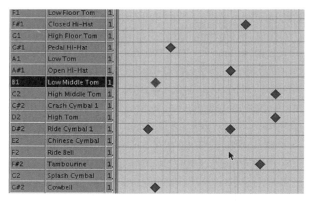

**MIDI notes in an editor designed for the programming of drum and percussion parts**

only the start of each note and either its pitch or the instrument that played it, or numerical values in a list.

Soon there were editors capable of displaying recorded MIDI messages as notes on a stave, and not long after that it became possible to use them print entire scores, as well as the parts for the individual instruments, complete with expression marks, guitar chord diagrams and lyrics.

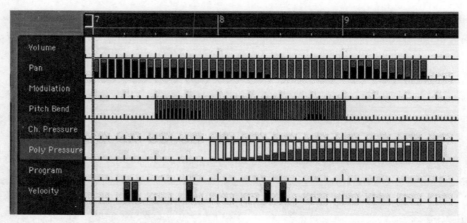

**An editor for MIDI control data, such as the movements of a modulation wheel or pedal**

The most important development that took place during the '90s was the gradual integration of both MIDI and audio data in sequencers, which were once seen as providing a MIDI-only environment. This began when some sequencers were programmed with the ability to store four to eight audio tracks along with the MIDI material, although at first you could do little more with these tracks than tweak their volume levels and position each individually in the stereo image.

Then Steinberg took things further with the development of its VST (Virtual Studio Technology) protocol and later its ASIO (Audio Stream Input/Output) driver architecture, which was designed for the use of multichannel audio hardware. At the same time, computers were getting faster at a breathtaking rate, making it possible for music software to integrate more and increasingly sophisticated functions. Soon the sequencers were able to manipulate many more audio tracks and provided tools for equalisation, then effects and, finally, plug-in instruments.

Today, the main sequencing applications, which have been constantly updated and enhanced over many years, have developed into comprehensive compositional and production environments for music and other audio projects. They offer sophisticated recording and editing functions for MIDI and audio data, integrated synths and samplers with sound banks for every conceivable musical genre, and of course all kinds of effects. They also have facilities for integrating video in a separate track, making it possible to use

them to compose soundtracks or add voiceovers and music to documentaries, and they even make it possible to collaborate with other musicians over the Internet, so you can transfer source files that can then be arranged, mixed and mastered in locations perhaps thousands of miles apart.

The functionality of these industry-leading audio sequencers can be expanded in a multitude of different ways via plug-ins supplying additional instruments or effects. Because the aim of these host programs is to be all things to all people, the main sequencers are huge applications with a vast range of functions, most of which many users will never need but which nonetheless need to be represented. As a result, the programs can be quite intimidating – and not only to beginners. However, they all follow the same basic pattern and are all similar to a certain degree. Of course, each uses different terminology to describe essentially the same things, and while there might be myriad differences of detail, with each product having its own strengths and weaknesses, if you can master any one of these applications, you can get the hang of another in a few days, if not a few hours.

If you haven't yet bought a software sequencer, you should ideally try out a demo of each of the leading programs to find out which best suits your way of working. You might even find – depending on your situation and the work you have in mind – that the best tool for you is something smaller and simpler. These alternatives will be looked at later, but for now let's take a look at the most widely used audio sequencers.

## Cubase

Along with Emagic's Logic, Steinberg's Cubase is one of the classic sequencing applications on the market today. (Both, incidentally, find their homes in Hamburg, but they're widely used all over the world.) Originally an independent company, Steinberg was taken over by Pinnacle Systems – a firm specialising in video software – at the beginning of 2003.

Cubase, which today comes in two flavours, SX and SL (the latter version having slightly reduced functionality), is a fully featured MIDI-plus-audio sequencer providing all the tools you need to make music on your computer, including a whole host of editors, synths, samplers and an integrated mixer offering a wide variety of effects. This virtual studio is fully expandable via a vast assortment of instrument and effects plug-ins based on Steinberg's own VST standard. At present, however, Cubase doesn't support Mac OS X's Audio Unit interface.

Launched at around the same time as Logic 6, Cubase SX and SL are radically overhauled versions of the application, both employing the same audio engine as Nuendo, Steinberg's media-production suite, which is designed for post-production and sound design in film and TV, as well as the handling of extended surround formats.

For more information, visit www.steinberg.de.

**Cubase SX**

## Logic

Logic is Cubase's prime competitor in the software-sequencer market and, like its rival, it has a long history, having originally been written for the Atari. In 2002, Emagic was taken over by Apple, which makes Logic and Mac OS X stablemates, in a sense.

Logic operates on the same fundamental principle as Cubase, any differences between the two programs being mostly superficial. Like Cubase, Logic manages MIDI and audio data simultaneously, offering an Arrange window along with a number of other editors, score-writing functions, a mixer, integrated tone generators and a wide variety of effects. Like Cubase, Logic is all the software you need for music production.

Being a subsidiary of Apple, Emagic naturally supports the Core Audio and Audio Unit standards, and with a certain proprietary zeal, it turns out, as VST plug-ins – supported under Mac Classic versions and still offered in the PC version – are no longer supported in the Mac OS X version. This is frustrating for many Logic users as, even if more and more plug-in manufacturers do now support the Audio Unit standard, there was certainly an argument in favour of Logic also supporting VST plug-ins. Fortunately, software manufacturers Fxpansion (www.fxpansion.com) have developed a program called VST to Audio Unit Adapter, which is a plug-in wrapper that allows users of Audio Unit-compatible applications such as Logic to integrate VST plug-ins and instruments seamlessly into their working environments.

At the beginning of 2004, Apple streamlined its Emagic professional audio-production software line, offering a choice of two sequencing packages: Logic Pro 6 for professional musicians and Logic Express 6 for students and teachers. As a general rule, you're best off buying the cheapest version of any sequencer until you're sure which one you need, and for three reasons:

1　You might find, after using the application for a few weeks, that you want to try another, in which case you don't want to have wasted a considerable amount of money;

2　Even the entry-level versions of the major sequencing applications offer a very wide range of functions and might well contain everything you need;

3　If you ever discover that there are functions in one of the larger versions of the program that you really do need, buying the entry-level model and upgrading to a higher-spec one generally won't cost that much more than buying the more expensive version in the first place.

**Emagic Logic**

## GarageBand

This software sequencer has been supplied free of charge for some time now with Macintoshes and is great for beginners. GarageBand is part of the iLife program bundle that retails separately for around £30 and also includes the programs iTunes, iMovie, iPhoto and iDVD.

GarageBand is an easy-to-use MIDI-plus-audio sequencer that's designed for absolute beginners and assumes no prior knowledge of music, let alone production techniques. It comes with more than 1,000 professionally recorded riffs – known as 'Apple Loops' – in a variety of moods and genres, taking the form of either MIDI phrases or audio loops, the tempo and/or pitch of which can then be modified using special software.

You can use these Apple Loops as building blocks for your own songs, changing their pitch and tempo and combining them with other Apple Loops to construct entire arrangements without ever touching an instrument. If you're feeling ambitious, you could even edit loops to create new variations, or connect a MIDI keyboard and create MIDI recordings via integrated software instruments and whatever other Audio Units are available. You could even use GarageBand to record audio.

As well as its tone generators, which are simplified derivatives of Logic instruments but nonetheless deliver excellent sounds, GarageBand boasts a wide range of effects including an equaliser, compressor, reverb, delay and a selection of virtual guitar amps,

all of which you can use to enhance the sound when you come to mix down. You can also adjust the volume and balance of each track individually and even fade tracks in or out.

GarageBand is designed to help beginners to unlock the Mac's potential for music production and has all the hallmarks of an Apple application, being elegant, well thought out, with a learning curve that won't have you pulling your hair out (which is more than can be said for most of the major sequencers) and a fun interface that brings swift rewards. It could even be used as a musical notepad or a mobile second sequencer for more seasoned users, although once they venture further into the realm of music production, GarageBand users will soon encounter its limitations. However, the developers were no doubt aware of this and have made the transition from GarageBand to Logic as smooth and painless as possible by allowing you to load GarageBand songs into Logic and edit or process them there.

For more information, visit www.apple.com/de/ilife/garageband/.

**GarageBand**

## Ableton Live

Compared to Cubase or Logic, Ableton Live is a very new and uncluttered piece of software, adopting a slightly different approach to that of the two classics.

As its name implies, with Live the emphasis is on improvisation and performance; it is a sequencer designed to be played like an instrument. Unlike its bigger brothers, Live currently has no MIDI capability,

## Ableton Live

focusing entirely on audio. There are therefore no integral tone generators; instead, the program plays back clips – drum loops and guitar licks from the clip library, for example, or those you've recorded yourself – that are stored as audio files on the hard disk. What turns Live into a sequencer is the manner in which these audio clips are triggered and arranged together.

As well as an Arrange view similar to that used by other sequencers, where tracks are stacked vertically, Live also has a Session view, which at first sight looks like a table, featuring a mixer-style channel strip above which tracks are arranged vertically in columns, with slots into which the audio clips can be loaded and played back with a mouse click.

In Live's Session view, audio clips can be combined spontaneously

Only one clip per channel can play back at any one time; each time you start a new clip, the clip that was playing previously on the same track is silenced. By combining different clips, organising them into scenes and starting and stopping them individually or in groups, you can create new arrangements quickly and easily. You can also choose whether the selected clips should start to play back at the beginning of the next bar or on the next quaver, so the tempo remains smooth and even.

Obviously, not all clips sound good together; two drum loops might be at different speeds, and tonal material from different clips might not be in the same key. However, any sequencer worth its salt will provide a remedy for such problems, and Live is no exception. What's so special about Live, though, is that the necessary adjustments can be performed in real time, and very flexibly. For instance, you can change the playback tempo of the clips (or groups thereof) that you're using without this affecting their pitch, as happens when you speed up or slow down the reels of a tape recorder. Conversely, you can change the pitch without this affecting the tempo. To a certain degree, these changes can even be effected without the results sounding unnatural, although you could use this way of working to transform the character of the material radically and produce something really weird and wonderful.

An interesting feature of Live is its so-called 'warp markers', which can be used to influence the tempo and rhythmic nature of an audio file. They can be used, for example, to match the tempos of two different audio clips, to straighten out rhythmic irregularities and to accelerate or decelerate the playback of audio events at any point in the piece.

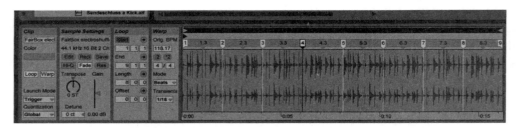

**Live's warp markers allow you to change the playback tempo and, with it, the timing and rhythm of the audio material**

Since Live was designed for stage use (although it can also be used to good effect in the studio), it also offers convenient recording facilities as well as live sampling and resampling functions. The instant-recording functions enable you to capture loops – phrases played by other members of the band, for example – on the fly and go directly from recording into loop playback, while with the resampling function you can record Live's own output.

Live also offers a number of integrated effects, and you can also use it with VST plug-ins – although here, of course, you're restricted to effects plug-ins, as there's no MIDI-sequencing function in Live to accommodate VST instruments.

For more information, visit www.ableton.com.

**Reason**

Created by Swedish company Propellerhead Software, Reason takes the idea of the virtual studio more literally than most, boasting an interface that contains a life-like representation of a rack stocked with synths, samplers and effects devices. Not only that but pressing the Tab key flips the rack around, enabling you to see the rear, with the devices connected by cables of various colours, allowing you to patch and repatch them freely by dragging the jacks from one socket to another with the mouse.

Actually, it's not strictly necessary to turn the rack around and connect the devices manually; Reason is perfectly capable of handling the signal routing automatically, as long as the devices are loaded into

**Reason's realistic interface allows you to repatch devices simply by dragging the jacks to different sockets**

the rack in the correct order. The devices supplied include various types of synth, samplers, a drum machine and a number of effects processors. Thanks to Reason's powerful signal-routing options, you can configure the rack exactly as you want it for each individual song.

Reason also contains an integrated and fully equipped software sequencer to control the devices in the rack. Here notes can either be entered from a MIDI keyboard or else programmed in using either the main or step sequencer, a pattern-based tool that's ideal for creating riffs and rhythm patterns.

**Reason's integrated sequencer (bottom) controls its rack of instruments (top)**

Live and Reason work together very well, as the former deals exclusively with audio tracks and the latter with MIDI, and indeed it's possible to use the ReWire interface (described earlier) to run the two programs in tandem, as explained later in this book.

For more information, visit www.propellerhead.se.

## Reaktor

This is another program you can use to create your own music-production environment.

Designed by Berlin-based company Native Instruments, Reaktor is a difficult application to pigeonhole; it's not a sequencer and it doesn't really fall into any of the other usual categories of music software. It's modular in structure, and you can construct any of a number of very different environments with a variety of different components, including amplifiers,

filters, oscillators, tape decks that can be used to record and play back audio from the hard disk, different types of control elements and displays. From these building blocks it's possible to construct any of a wide variety of instruments, effects and devices that can be combined and configured in all kinds of different ways.

Available for both Mac and Windows, Reaktor has an army of devotees forever developing and publishing new instruments and ensembles for it. In fact, the Native Instruments website hosts a library allowing you to download or upload new creations, and well over 1,000 such devices have been created already. Reaktor fans are creative, and there's a huge and diverse range of new instruments available for it free of charge. Native Instruments also hosts its own library of selected examples and every now and again publishes new sets of instruments.

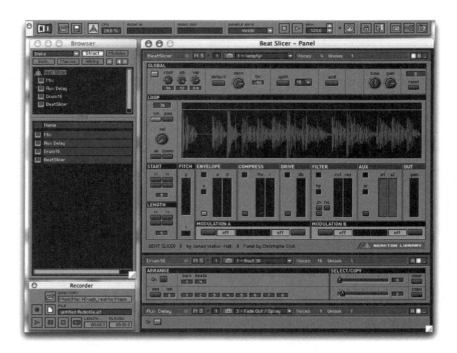

**Boasting hundreds of instruments, Reaktor has many faces**

If you're ambitious, you can use Reaktor to create custom-made instruments and studio environments capable of deputising for a sequencer and its plug-ins, as well as providing tailor-made solutions for live performance. Instead of running Reaktor as a stand-

alone program, many users employ it as a VST or Audio Unit plug-in to be used in a sequencer, thus making it possible for Reaktor to combine audio and MIDI tracks.

However, for users with neither the time nor the inclination to contend with Reaktor's modules but who

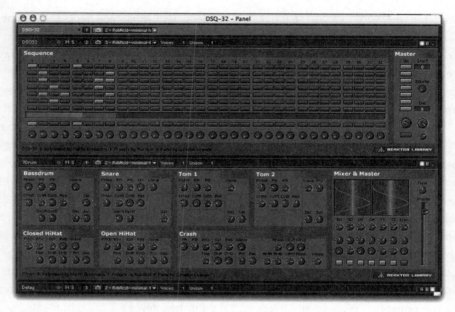

**Reaktor: drum machine, synth or effects device?**

nevertheless want to work with Reaktor's instruments, Native Instruments' Reaktor Session is a more affordable version of the same program enabling you to load and use Reaktor ensembles, although you can't use it to modify them or create instruments of your own.

For more information, visit www.native-instruments.de.

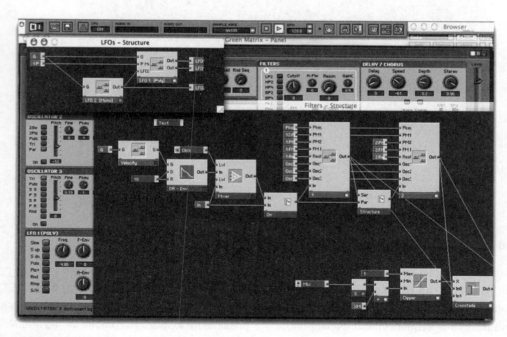

**Reaktor's modular nature means you can use it in any number of roles**

## Other Programs

As well as the major software sequencers covered here, there are a number of other programs worthy of note, even though they might be less widely used.

Mark Of The Unicorn's Digital Performer, for instance, can handle both audio and MIDI tracks and is very similar in terms of overall design to Cubase and Logic. The Mac OS X version of Digital Performer supports both Core Audio and Audio Units, while under Mac OS 9 MOTU also offers a plug-in interface of its own called MAS (MOTU Audio System). For more information, visit www.motu.com.

**MOTU Digital Performer**

Meanwhile, Digidesign (www.digidesign.com) has also traditionally played an important role in professional music production on the Mac. Its market-leading Pro Tools system is based on a combination of an audio sequencer with an associated MIDI section and special PCI cards that provide additional processing power, as well as connection options for proprietary audio interfaces.

The Pro Tools systems that were widely used under

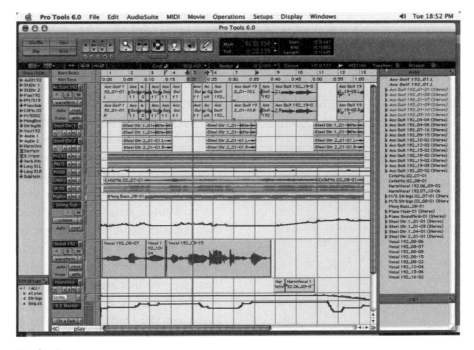

**Digidesign Pro Tools 6**

Mac OS 9 are now also available for Mac OS X from version 6 onwards, but since they're somewhat expensive, their use is mainly confined to professional production environments. However, Pro Tools also offers a plug-in interface of its own, known as TDM, and plug-ins supporting this standard are processed using the DSPs of Digidesign hardware and therefore impose little or no strain on the host CPU.

Digidesign also produces a number of more affordable hardware solutions with audio inputs and outputs that are used with Pro Tools LE, a modified version of Pro Tools that employs a second plug-in interface, called RTAS. Pro Tools LE is also now available for Mac OS X, as is Pro Tools Free, a demo version of the program capable of running on Windows and Macintosh systems without Digidesign hardware.

These Digidesign systems are particularly noteworthy because of their high audio quality and because the Pro Tools software has a proven track record, but I won't discuss them any further here because Digidesign hardware can only be used with Digidesign software and vice versa, whereas this book is more concerned with exploring the many possibilities accorded by the Mac OS X platform in general for combining applications and hardware of different kinds and from different sources.

Another piece of software you might find useful is Max/MSP, a graphic programming environment for music,

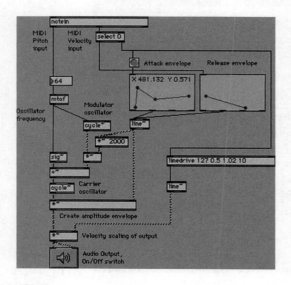

**Max/MSP**

audio and multimedia developed by Cycling 74 (www.cycling74.com). Like Reaktor, Max/MSP is a modular system that can be used to create all kinds of instruments and devices, offering users enormous freedom in the way they choose to make music with the computer.

Max/MSP's potential goes far beyond the area of making music and includes the ability to edit video in real time. The program's modular nature is more pronounced than Reaktors, and its charms are somewhat more esoteric – for example, you can write your own objects in C++ and integrate them into the system, which is great if you can do it but slightly too much like rocket science for most users!

## Effects And Synth Plug-ins
### What Are Plug-ins And What Are They For?

Plug-ins are program modules that can be integrated into a larger host application in order to expand its functionality and enhance its sound palette. Today, every leading sequencer offers a plug-in interface whose protocol is then made available to third-party designers of effects and software instruments so that they, too, can contribute new functions and features to the host application. There's a mouthwatering variety of plug-ins currently available for all the main sequencing applications, some produced by the manufacturer but most developed by software houses specialising in designing plug-ins, often working in collaboration with the manufacturers of hardware sequencers and effects devices. There are also many plug-ins available in the form of freeware and shareware.

Plug-ins can be divided into two broad categories: effects (audio in/audio out) and instruments (MIDI in/audio out). However, the difference is only of any consequence if you're working with Ableton Live as, although this program supports the VST interface, it has no MIDI-sequencing capabilities and so can't do anything with instrument plug-ins, which can only be used in connection with MIDI-input devices. If you're using Live, therefore, you'll only really be interested in those plug-ins that accept audio signals as their input.

In many cases, a plug-in is simply the software equivalent of a hardware studio device that performs a single clearly defined task, such as a compressor, expander, equaliser or reverb. With other plug-ins,

**This is where Mac OS X keeps all installed plug-ins, making them available to all compatible applications**

however, the operating principles of two or more such devices have been combined to produce something entirely new, while others have been designed differently from the ground up and have no hardware equivalents in the studio.

What follows is a brief introduction to a number of manufacturers of plug-ins that offer particularly high-quality, useful or original solutions.

## Effects Plug-in Manufacturers
### Waves

The Israel-based company Waves has for years been producing plug-ins for a variety of interfaces and platforms. Since August 2003, its new products can also be used as Audio Unit host applications under Mac OS X. The company produces high-quality compressors and equalisers as well as a good reverb and some outstandingly creative effects plug-ins.

Waves' Renaissance series has a particularly good reputation, featuring software versions of classic studio devices, while its mastering plug-ins are also very popular, including the L1 limiter, which is used to enhance the intensity and perceived loudness of recordings.

Waves plug-ins are offered in a variety of bundles, the largest being the Platinum bundle, which comprises some 25 different plug-ins and retails for around £1,875. Quality seldom comes cheap, of course, and Waves plug-ins are state of the art. For more information, visit www.waves.com.

### PSP

Up-and-coming Polish company PSP Audioware also does a nice line in plug-ins, including good delay effects, a tape-saturation effect known as Vintage Warmer and a free level-meter plug-in.

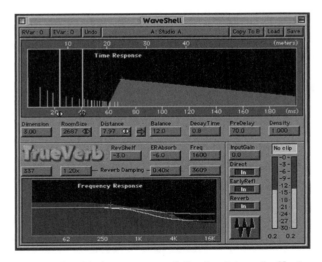

**Waves TrueVerb was one of the best loved effects plug-ins under Mac OS 9**

**PSP's Vintage Warmer transfers the warmth of analogue recordings to the digital world**

61

Virtually all PSP plug-ins, including MasterQ (a parametric equaliser), EasyVerb (a reverb) and Nitro (a multi-mode filter), now offer both VST and Audio Unit support under Mac OS X, with the exception of the Lexicon PSP 42 (a digital stereo delay and phrase sampler), which supports VST only. For more information, visit www.pspaudioware.com.

## GRM Tools

The next stop in our tour of the plug-in world is France, where the Groupe de Recherches Musicales of the Institut National Audiovisuel – which has long been a leading force in the development of electronic music – is fast establishing a reputation for the outstanding quality of its plug-ins. Currently, GRM Tools provide 14 different processors for creating special effects with sound samples including high-power filtering, time stretching, harmonisation and noise gating, as well as more unusual and, in some cases, unique functions such as a Doppler effect along with plug-ins for comb filtering, time freezing, micro-random shuffling, additive synthesis and more.

**GRM Tools produce some extraordinary effects that are now available for Mac OS X**

The plug-ins produced by GRM comprise a variety of organic-sounding delay, filter, resonator and granular effects, and when using them you have the ability to morph at any time between different presets as quickly or as slowly as you like. For more information, visit www.grmtools.org.

## Prosoniq

The plug-ins developed by the German supplier Prosoniq proved popular on other platforms, and now they've been ported to Mac OS X. One classic is the Orange Vocoder, which can be used to produce futuristic-sounding vocal harmonies, robotic voices and much else besides. A tone generator is provided to serve as the carrier.

The highly rated North Pole plug-in, meanwhile, offers a resonant filter with a resonance control like those found in analogue synths, as well as envelope followers for the input signal, distortion and delay. Sounds exciting? Then try it out; there's a copy on the accompanying CD.

**The North Pole, a freeware plug-in from Prosoniq that generates filter effects**

The Prosoniq range includes many other interesting plug-ins such as Ambisone, which enables you to position a sound source in three dimensions using a normal stereo playback system; the mastering plug-in Dynasone; and the Roomulator reverb. The Mac OS X version of Prosoniq's plug-ins are in VST format. For more information, visit www.prosoniq.net.

**The Prosoniq Voxciter offers a wide range of functions for the processing of vocal recordings**

## Smartelectronix

It's worth mentioning Smartelectronix here as its plug-ins are either freeware or donationware, which means you can decide for yourself how much (if anything) to pay for them. A large number of independent software engineers use Smartelectronix to distribute their plug-ins, some of which will run under Mac OS X.

While it's well worth browsing through all Smartelectronix products, Mac OS X users should take special note of the supplier Destroy FX, whose range includes a large number of unusual plug-ins for the platform including Buffer Override, which can be used to produce strange echo, stuttering and granular effects. Destroy FX's Mac OS X range is made up entirely of Audio Unit plug-ins.

**The Smartelectronix range includes all manner of oddball plug-ins**

The effects supplied by Smartelectronix aren't always what you'd call 'mainstream', and a normal supplier would perhaps have difficulty earning money from all of them, but the site is nonetheless well worth checking out as there's always plenty going on there and the plug-ins can be downloaded for free. For more information, visit www.smartelectronix.com.

## MDA

Maxim Digital Audio is an English firm that allows Mac OS X users to download no fewer than 34 effects plug-ins free of charge. All are in VST format, and while they might not always look pretty, tending to lack the colourful controls and displays typical of most commercial plug-ins, they do sound good and cover a wide spectrum of effects.

The MDA range includes conventional effects such as compressors, limiters, filters and distortion, but also more complex plug-ins such as a multi-band compressor, two different vocoders, a plug-in to replace the drum sounds in an audio signal with synthetic ones, a sub-bass synth and many more.

Although MDA has been giving away plug-ins for some time now for older Mac operating systems, Windows and even BeOS, there's nothing amateurish about their product and the company has been commissioned by high-calibre companies like Steinberg and Expansion to develop instruments. For more information, visit www.mda-vst.com.

## Native Instruments

Berlin-based software manufacturer Native Instruments is one of the highest-profile suppliers of music-production applications. I've already mentioned its modular system, Reaktor, which can also be run as a plug-in, offering a wide potential for effects creation.

Over the last few years, the Native Instruments range has expanded rapidly, though the emphasis is still on software instruments rather than effects, as the company's name suggests. Nonetheless, NI does produce two effects that should be mentioned here: the Spektral Delay and the Vokator. Both are based on real-time FFT (Fast Fourier Transform) technology, which involves slicing an audio system into a large number of small frequency bands and then applying processing and gain to each band individually.

The Spektral Delay plug-in enables you to program the level, delay time and amount of feedback for up to 160 different frequency bands per stereo channel as well as apply various modulation effects to the signal. It's possible to achieve extraordinary results this way, from subtle spatial effects to rhythmic cascades of overtones and dense atmospheric sounds. The plug-in's more extreme settings are more appropriate for experimental music, but it also offers more subtle settings; for example, unlike conventional filters, you can adjust the amplitude level of all 160 bands simply by using the mouse to draw in the desired frequency response, which can take any shape. Using

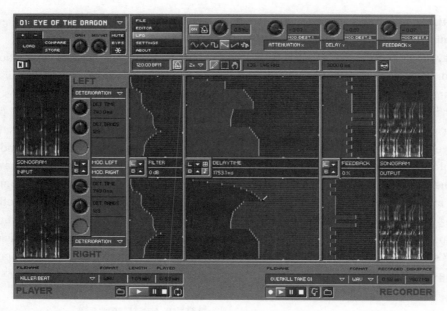

**Native Instruments' Spektral Delay, coming soon to Mac OS X**

the Spektral Delay, it's possible to remove entire bands, leaving their neighbours unattenuated. Filter curves can be drawn for each channel separately or shared. Like all NI products, the Spektral Delay is available in both VST and Audio Unit formats.

Because it's brand new, NI's Vokator naturally supports Mac OS X. This plug-in is an FFT implementation of the vocoder principle, whereby the sound characteristics of one signal (the modulator) are applied to another (the carrier) by controlling the

**NI Vokator**

amplitude of different frequency bands. Thanks to the real-time FFT technology involved, instead of the 40 or so bands offered by conventional vocoders employing band-pass filters, the Vokator splits the signal into 1,024 different frequency bands for both analysis and synthesis.

The Vokator also includes a tone-generation section, the carrier signal for which is either supplied by a synth or granular sampler or an external signal. Meanwhile, the modulator can be either an external signal or an audio recording played back by a tape deck. As well as every conceivable Vocoder function, the Vokator offers a spectral level for signal manipulation. Like the Spektral Delay, the Vokator is a complex effect whose full potential remains unexplored.

For more information about Native Instruments products, visit www.native-instruments.de.

### TC Works

No list of important plug-in suppliers for Mac OS X would be complete without a mention of TC Works, a company that has a fine reputation on both the Apple and PC platforms for top-notch compressors, reverbs and chorus effects, all of which are based on the algorithms developed by TC Electronics, a Danish company that specialises in the manufacture of studio devices.

The Mac OS X version of TC Works' best-selling package, the Native Bundle, comprises six high-quality compressor, filter, reverb and equaliser plug-ins, integrated via the VST interface.

For more information, visit www.tcworks.de.

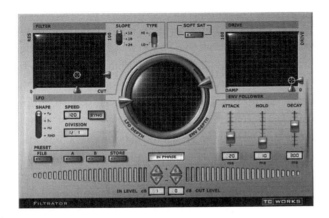

**TC Works' Filtrator**

# Synth Plug-in Manufacturers
## Apple

No, you're not hallucinating – Apple really *has* produced a software instrument of its own. The DLS Music plug-in comes bundled with Mac OS X and is a simple sample player with 128 different sounds arranged in accordance with the General MIDI protocol.

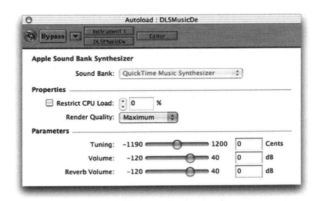

**The DLS Music synth, an unassuming sample player whose sounds can be selected and played via MIDI**

Admittedly, DLS Music has no really mind-blowing sounds, and the parameters don't extend much beyond being able to modify the tuning, volume and intensity of the integrated reverb, but you can hardly look a gift horse in the mouth, and besides, one or two of the sounds could come in useful from time to time. DLS Music can be used by any AU-compatible host program, including, of course, Logic.

### Native Instruments

As well as Reaktor and the two effects plug-ins I described earlier, Native Instruments has a number of instrument plug-ins in its range. As I mentioned a while ago, Native Instruments supports both VST and Audio Units formats, and the company's plug-ins will therefore function with all of the most important host applications.

Another advantage of Native Instruments' tone generators and effects is that they can invariably be run not only as plug-ins but also as stand-alone programs, which means you can play their instruments using your MIDI keyboard without needing to load a sequencer first, while Reaktor can operate as a fully autonomous production environment.

There's a wide selection of very good instruments available for both Reaktor and Reaktor Session (Reaktor's lite counterpart), and Native Instruments is constantly adding to these with their own instrument sets, so even if the modular nature of these kinds of applications holds little appeal, the fact that they provide access to this huge instrument library is enough to make them an interesting investment.

Native Instruments has also established a reputation for its lovingly crafted emulations of legendary instruments, such as the Pro 53 – one of the most famous of all analogue synthesisers – and the Hammond organ, the software version of which even simulates the valve distortion and rotating Leslie speakers of the original.

**Native Instruments' B4 recreates the much-loved Hammond sound**

Another classic instrument to be revived by Native Instruments in software form is Yamaha's DX7, one of the biggest selling synths of all time. NI's version, the FM7, is not only capable of reproducing the DX7's entire stock of factory presets but also allows you to load thousands of patches created for the instrument over the years. In fact, the FM7 surpasses the original in many respects and is both a very modern and a very powerful software synth.

Along with the synthesiser, the sampler is a virtually indispensable component of any modern hardware or software studio because of its enormous versatility. From generating loops for hip-hop or dance music to

providing lush orchestral sounds for film scores, the sampler is capable of answering the needs of the most diverse musical genres – and, of course, Native Instruments have that base covered, too.

In fact, the company offers not just one but an entire series of software samplers, each catering to different needs. The top-of-the-range model is a lavishly equipped program called Kontakt, which not only comes supplied with a large sound library of its own but is also compatible with the sample libraries of many of the other main suppliers.

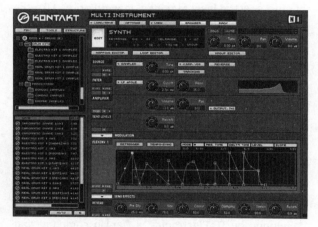

**Kontakt, Native Instruments' flagship sampler**

Kontakt is semi-modular, but even so it's fairly simple to operate. It allows you to modify samples in various ways, giving a sufficiently wide sound palette to cover many different applications. The granular samples offer particular scope for creativity, as it's possible to vary their tempo and pitch independently.

Kontakt is complemented by Kompakt, a non-modular version of the same sampler without the granular functions. Meanwhile, a third sampler, Intakt, specialises in the playback and manipulation of loops, while Battery is optimised for working with drum samples. Both of the latter two devices can run as stand-alone programs or as an Audio Units or VST 2 plug-ins.

Finally, I must mention Absynth 2, a soft synth that supports Core Audio, Core MIDI and Audio Units under Mac OS X. This device also features a semi-modular tone-generation section with which it's possible to produce some captivating, organic sounds. Version 2

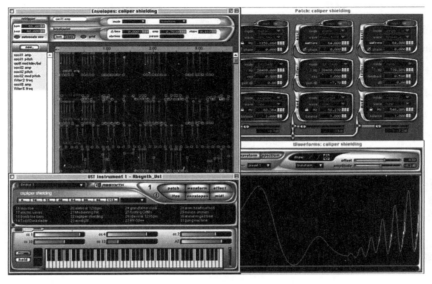

**Absynth 2's complex envelopes allow you to produce independent rhythmic sound textures**

also offers a sample-playing facility that even includes granular functions.

One of Absynth's special features is its complex, multilayered envelopes with which it's possible to produce all kinds of rhythmic modulations. Absynth also allows you to construct waveforms by summing partials as well as by drawing them in with the mouse.

For more information, visit www.native-instruments.de.

## Steinberg

Steinberg is another heavy-hitter in the field of software instruments with a large and constantly growing range of plug-ins available, some produced in-house, some created in collaboration with other software houses and some developed entirely by third-party suppliers.

Regardless of their origin, all plug-ins provided by Steinberg are in VST format, which means you can load them from within Cubase (for example) but not from within Logic. However, unlike Native Instruments' plug-ins, Steinberg's can't be run as stand-alone applications, only through a VST-compatible host program.

One of the most important instruments in the Steinberg range is HALion, a sampler for which an increasingly large range of sounds is available. HALion might not have the flexibility of NI's Kontakt, whose modular construction and granular synthesis gives it

an edge for experimental music, but HALion's audio quality is excellent and its sounds are varied enough to cover virtually all applications.

Steinberg also offers a number of special editions of HALion that are tailored for particular instruments or instrument groups. The Grand, for instance, is a plug-in equipped with a large number of high-quality grand-piano samples, while the HALion String Edition contains a 5GB library of string samples, the Virtual Guitarist features idiomatic guitar chords and licks sampled from electric and acoustic instruments, and Groove Agent offers a wide variety of drum sounds and styles.

Steinberg also has the market for synth plug-ins well covered. The Plex restructuring synth, for example, employs an innovative tone-generation system and an intuitive interface featuring a dial consisting of a number of concentric rings that can be rotated individually, allowing you to select the low-frequency components of one instrument, the high-frequency components of a second and the envelope of a third. Using this system, you can create a hybrid with the acoustic foundation of a grand piano, the high-frequency components of a flute and the envelope of a guitar, for example. The tone generation is based on samples, the sounds are surprisingly good and it's easy

**Steinberg's HALion 2 sampler (top) and Plex synth (bottom) plug-ins**

to come up with novel yet musical sounds. However, if you're more interested in creating weird effects or experimental music, there are other instruments on the market better suited to your needs; while it might include a number of surprising permutations, Plex's sound set is essentially finite.

Meanwhile, the D'cota VST synth – a close cousin of the VirSyn Tera discussed later – offers even greater creative freedom, employing three different tone-generation systems: one analogue, one based on additive synthesis and the third on a system similar to that of physical modelling. The additive-synthesis section is particularly interesting as it can be used to create some beautiful, scintillating sounds.

For more information about Steinberg products, visit www.steinberg.net.

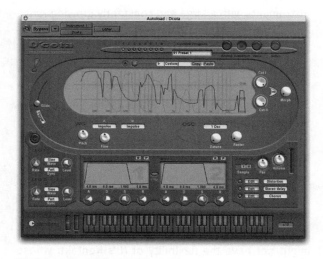

**Steinberg's D'cota VST synth**

### Emagic

The creators of the Logic software sequencer, Emagic also makes good software instruments, but whereas those of its competitor, Steinberg, can be used in any VST host, not just Cubase, almost all Emagic instruments can be used only with Logic. Even though they might operate like plug-ins, they're essentially parts of Logic itself and are unlocked upon purchase. Like Cubase, Logic comes with a number of relatively simple instruments, but the larger, more powerful ones discussed here cost extra.

One of the most important instruments in the Emagic range is the EXS24 sampler, which boasts an impressive array of features and is compatible with a wide range of sample library formats, including EXS24 native, Akai, GigaSampler, SampleCell II, SoundFont2 and REX2. Emagic recently introduced the EXS24 Mk II, which features the same matrix as the ES2 (see below), providing comprehensive routing possibilities and a multimode filter.

**Emagic's EXS24 Mk II sampler features a modulation matrix and support for a wide range of sample formats**

Emagic also have an impressive range of soft synths, including the ES1, which offers a simple but well-thought-out architecture, a powerful sound and quick, responsive envelopes that produce convincing results even with percussive sounds, which is more than can be said for most synthesisers. However, while the ES1 is efficient and very useful, if you want something a little more subtle, its stablemate the ES2 offers a far larger number of sound and modulation parameters, allowing you to achieve more sophisticated results.

Emagic's range also features plug-ins that emulate real instruments as well as synthesisers. The EVB3, for example, is a virtual Hammond organ that even reproduces the effect of rotating Leslie speakers and the characteristic distortion of the original.

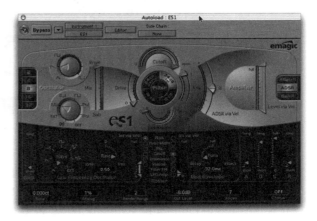

**ES1 offers a simple and well-thought-out tone-generation architecture as well as great sounds**

Meanwhile, the EVD6 is a virtual version of the Hohner Clavinet D6, an instrument made popular through featuring on Stevie Wonder's hit 'Superstition'. The algorithms used to reconstruct this instrument's funky, clavichord-like twang can also be used to turn the EVD6 into a highly versatile synth producing all kinds of interesting string and percussion sounds. Distortion, phaser and wah-wah effects – all typical of the D6 – are also integrated.

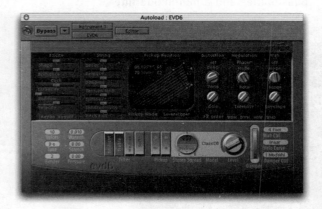

**Logic EVD6**

In the same retrospective vein, Emagic's EVP88 emulates the legendary Fender Rhodes electric piano.

In fact, the plug-in offers 12 emulations of various Fenders, Wurlitzers, etc, whose sound can be changed drastically. The Vintage Piano EVP73, meanwhile, is a cut-down version of the same plug-in, emulating only the one Fender model.

For more information about Emagic products, visit www.emagic.de.

## Waldorf

Waldorf established its reputation with hardware synths like the Microwave; its larger successor, the Wave; the analogue Pulse; and the virtual analogue Q. Like its successors, 1989's Microwave employed a system known as *wavetable synthesis*, the brainchild of Wolfgang Palm, who went on to found PPG. On his departure, Waldorf developed wavetable technology further.

Nowadays, Waldorf focuses on producing plug-ins, one of which, the PPG Wave 2.V, is modelled on the legendary PPG wavetable synths. The plug-in faithfully recreates the sounds of the originals, which had a defining influence upon the music of the early '80s, and it appears that they're still popular today, as the plug-in is also available in VST format for Mac OS X.

**Waldorf's PPG Wave plug-in**

Waldorf's other plug-in instrument, a drum synth called Attack, is also very popular; so popular, in fact, that only a few months after the company released the plug-in, Waldorf released a hardware version, tracing the developmental curve in reverse!

Attack is a synth designed for the creation of classic analogue and electronic drum and percussion sounds. Each kit contains up to 24 sounds – 12 unpitched and 12 melodic – which are generated by either one or two oscillators, each of which offers six analogue waveforms and three sampled ones. Although samplers are more commonly used to provide drum and percussion sounds in sequencer-based environments, Attack's pre-programmed kits prove that more vibrant and interesting results can be achieved through synthesis.

For more information about Waldorf's products, visit www.waldorf-gmbh.de.

**Waldorf's Attack is designed for the creation of electronic drum and percussion sounds**

## VirSyn

Masterminded by Harry Gohs, VirSyn produces the Tera synth, on which Steinberg's D'cota is based. However, unlike the D'cota, which is compatible only with the VST interface, the Tera can also operate as an Audio Unit plug-in or even in stand-alone mode.

**The Tera's characteristic interface featuring XY control elements**

While a software synth is usually used as a plug-in within a host program that lets you record and edit the MIDI messages directed to it, the Tera can also be used as a software synth in its own right, as it provides the facility for entering melodies and creating arrangements via its own powerful step sequencer. It's a multitimbral synth capable of playing back 16 different sounds simultaneously, each controlled by a separate sequence.

While Steinberg's D'cota (which, incidentally, was also largely designed by Harry Gohs) gives you the facility to switch between three different tone-generation processes, the Tera is totally modular in structure, allowing you to combine the processes of different modules in order to create the desired sound. This hands-on approach to programming might seem a very complex way of working, but in fact the Tera is more intuitive than Native Instruments' Reaktor, say. Even so, the sequencer comes with a large library of ready-programmed sounds, so users can benefit from the results of modularity without getting their hands dirty.

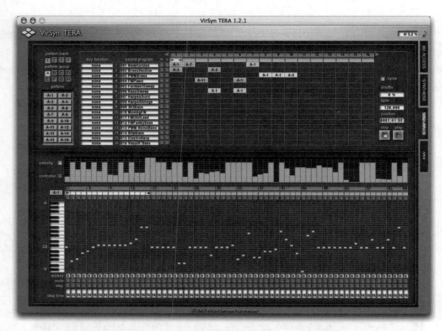

**The Tera's sequencer can control up to 16 different sounds simultaneously**

The Tera is very versatile, and if your computer is fast enough you can produce fine-sounding arrangements with it alone. The only limiting factor is that, because it's a pure-bred synth, it can't play samples. However, it has a number of above-average integrated effects that provide a useful complement to the tonal sounds.

Meanwhile, the other synth in the VirSyn range, the Cube, supports the same set of interfaces as the Tera but isn't modular in structure, being restricted to using additive synthesis (see Chapter 1, 'The Fundamentals') for the creation of its sounds. What is remarkable about it, however, is its elegance and ease of use, with morphing functions combining with a vast array of parameters to offer intuitive access to a wealth of sounds. The Cube can be used to create vibrant, dynamic and sometimes completely new timbres and transients.

For more information on VirSyn products, visit www.virsyn.com.

**VirSyn Cube**

## reFX

reFX boasts a wide range of interesting and affordable VST instruments, including analogue emulators such as the Juno X2, which is modelled on the popular Roland Juno, and the PlastiCZ, which employs a new variety of FM synthesis.

**reFX's PlastiCZ has a full-bodied sound and looks even prettier in colour**

However, it's the QuadraSID that seems most likely to acquire cult status, emulating the sound chip of the legendary Commodore C-64 home computer to produce a range of superb, if somewhat idiosyncratic sounds. Strictly speaking, the QuadraSID emulates four of these sound chips to deliver a far fuller sound, while it also offers a number of features that were never available on the Commodore, such as four LFOs and an arpeggiator.

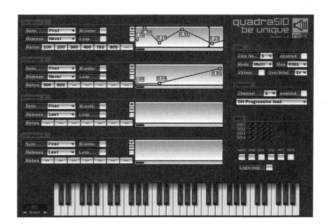

**The QuadraSID's Envelope page**

reFX also has guitar sounds nicely covered with the Slayer 2 plug-in, a VST plug-in available for Mac OS X that combines physically modelled guitar sounds with an amp simulator and a huge arsenal of effects of which up to 16 can be used simultaneously.

For more information about reFX products, visit www.refx.net.

## GMedia Music

GMedia is a company well known for its successful emulation the Mellotron, an instrument that enjoyed a somewhat ephemeral popularity in the '60s and produced its sounds via the use of audio tapes. For each key, there was a separate tape containing a recording of an acoustic instrument playing the equivalent note, and when you pressed the key, you heard the tape playing back. With this technique, the Mellotron was able to produce what at the time seemed breathtakingly authentic string, flute and choir sounds and plenty else besides. However, there was a big drawback in that the only way to switch from one sound to another was to change the tapes.

In today's age of ruthless digital accuracy, the Mellotron's imperfections are a large part of its charm; wear and tear on the mechanical parts introduced an element of unpredictability along with a tendency for the sound to waver in pitch.

Beginning with a pure emulator, the M-Tron, GMedia decided to go further and produce the Megatron, a deluxe version of the instrument with new components such as filters, envelopes and a stock of virtual audio tapes far larger than that found in the original Mellotron.

**GMedia's Megatron is the deluxe version of the virtual Mellotron**

Meanwhile, GMedia's Oddity emulates another classic analogue synth: the once-popular Arp Odyssey. Like all of GMedia's plug-in instruments, it requires a VST 2.0-compatible host that supports VST instruments or a Mac OS X application that supports Audio Units.

For more information about GMedia's products, visit www.gmediamusic.com.

## Arturia

One plug-in that's held in particularly high esteem is French firm Arturia's Moog Modular V, which is an emulation of the Moog 3C, an early modular synth designed by Bob Moog and much prized at the time for its full, warm sound, its outstanding filters and its very fast envelopes. Even today, the 3C is regarded as the very epitome of good synth design.

**The Moog 3C, the original modular system**

Arturia's award-winning Moog Modular V offers not only an eye-catching visual approximation of the 3C's impressive user interface but also a loving true analogue emulation of its sound characteristics. It comes complete with over 400 presets created by well-known sound designers and runs as a stand-alone program in its own right or as a VST or Audio Unit plug-in.

For more information about Arturia's products, visit www.arturia.com.

## Want More?

This survey of currently available effects and synth plug-ins on the market is in no way comprehensive, being a purely subjective selection of some of the most important suppliers and their software. In any case, it would be impossible to cover every supplier, never mind every last one of their products, since the market is in constant flux, with the shareware and freeware sectors being particularly active and new products entering the market on an almost daily basis.

If you want to keep up to date with what's available on the plug-in market, you're best off subscribing to a magazine specialising in computer-assisted music production and making regular visits to the websites of the leading suppliers, as well as those maintained by enthusiasts. The Appendix contains a list of the most important website addresses.

## Sample Editors
### What Are They And What Do They Do?

So far, we've looked and MIDI-plus-audio sequencers and analogous production environments, along with the effects and instrument plug-ins designed to enhance them. However, there's a type of application that hasn't been covered yet but which also plays an important role in computer-based music production.

Sample editors are primarily designed for the editing, processing and mastering of audio files. They can be used, for example, to remove silence from the beginning of an audio file, to make quiet sounds louder, to correct errors, to remove noise, to apply fade-ins, fade-outs and crossfades, to add compression and much else besides.

Now, you might be arguing at this point that you don't need a special program to do all this, since all of these tasks can be performed within an audio sequencer, as long as you have the right plug-ins, and of course you'd be right. However, there's one important difference: when you edit or process audio tracks from within an audio sequencer, you're almost invariably working non-destructively – ie the original audio file remains unaltered. All your edits do is alter the way the audio sounds on playback, with the sequencer implementing your modifications in real time each time you hit Play.

Of course, it's possible to record (ie *render*) the results of all the editing and processing that has been applied to a track so that you don't need a computer to implement the changes you introduced, but you might not want to create a second file. Besides, audio sequencers are designed for the recording and editing of entire songs and even orchestral works, with perhaps dozens of different instruments in the mix, not for working with short samples, so using a synth as though it was a sample editor is rather like cracking a nut with a sledgehammer.

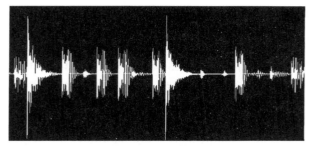

**Graphic representation of a digital recording**

Of course, if the sequencer offers an integrated sample editor that allows you to edit destructively (ie irreversibly), as some of the best sequencers do, these objections don't apply, although it should be noted that stand-alone sample editors tend to be more powerful and easier to work with than those integrated into sequencers. Also, no two sample editors adopt the same approach, so you might prefer to use different editors for different tasks.

You might find the greater power of a specialist sample editor useful when, for instance, you want to perform the same task or set of tasks on all the files in a folder (what's known as *batch editing*), whereby you can specify a set of operations to be performed on a set of files and then leave the application to do all the processing automatically. For example, you might want to normalise a group of samples (ie find their highest level before running into clipping), brighten them (by boosting the higher frequencies) and then save them in a different audio format. With a sequencer, you'd probably have to load each file in turn – which could get very tedious very quickly if there were 40 or 50 of them – and perform the same set of operations over and over again. With a powerful sample editor, however, you could do the whole lot in one go.

This section looks at some of the most powerful OS X-compatible sample editors and describes some of their features. There are also similar applications available as shareware or freeware, although these are invariably simpler and offer less functionality.

### Spark

Produced by TC Works, this is a tried-and-tested sample editor that's available in three versions: XL,

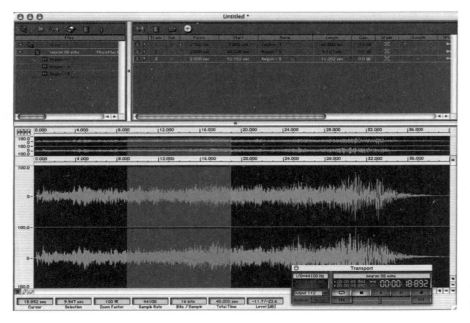

**TC Works'
Spark ME**

SE Plus and ME, the latter of which is free but nonetheless useful.

Spark offers an intuitive one-window user interface whereby the top left-hand corner of the screen shows a list of the audio files to be edited and the segments within them selected by the user, while the bottom half of the screen displays the waveform of the selected segment. The top right-hand corner, meanwhile, shows a playlist where you can reorder the audio segments before recording them to CD.

You've probably guessed from this brief description that Spark's special strengths lie in the area of mastering, and indeed it features various processing and analysis functions to help with this task. The XL version is particularly useful here, coming complete with a full box of tools for applying the finishing touches to audio files. Thanks to the various effects that come bundled with it and its compatibility with VST effects plug-ins, Spark is an excellent editor not only for mastering but also for general sound-design work. The two larger versions of the program also allow you to load QuickTime videos and add sound to them.

For more information about TC Works' products, visit www.tcworks.de.

## Peak

Developed by Bias, Peak is another fully equipped program designed for the editing of audio data. Like Spark, it offers a wide range of editing functions, plug-in integration (VST and, from version 4 onwards, Audio Units), a playlist, CD-writing functions, batch processing and the like.

With Peak, however, the emphasis is rather different. Whereas Spark is designed more for mastering entire pieces and assembling material for a CD, Peak is optimised for the editing of samples for use with samplers. For example, unlike Spark, it enables you to create sample loops, which reduce the storage requirements of samples both in RAM and on the hard disk. It can also exchange sample data with a hardware sampler via SCSI, so you can use it to edit the samples used by the machine. In fact, this is a big selling point, but only if you actually use a hardware sampler, of course, and then only if your Mac has a SCSI interface.

Aside from these differences, there's little to choose between the two programs, so you're best off trying them both and then deciding which one's best for you.

Peak comes in four different versions, the largest of which, Peak TDM, is designed primarily for use with

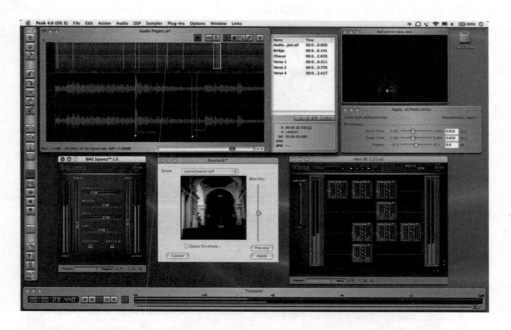

**Bias Peak 4 has the same brushed-titanium look as the Power Book**

Digidesign's Pro Tools. Then come Peak, Peak DV (which costs half as much as Peak) and Peak LE (which costs half as much as Peak DV), with the range of functions and price of each application shrinking accordingly. The DV version is specially designed for video editing.

For more information about Bias products, visit www.bias-inc.com.

## Melodyne

Developed by Celemony, Melodyne is a highly original program offering fascinating possibilities. At first

sight it looks like an audio sequencer, having several tracks for audio files, arrange functions and a small mixer. However, that's where the similarity ends; the arrange functions are, in fact, incidental to the program's main purpose.

Melodyne was designed primarily for the detailed editing of monophonic material, such as lead vocals, saxophone and flute solos (although it's also extremely useful for editing drum loops). What makes the program remarkable is that it allows you to edit audio material as easily as if it was MIDI data.

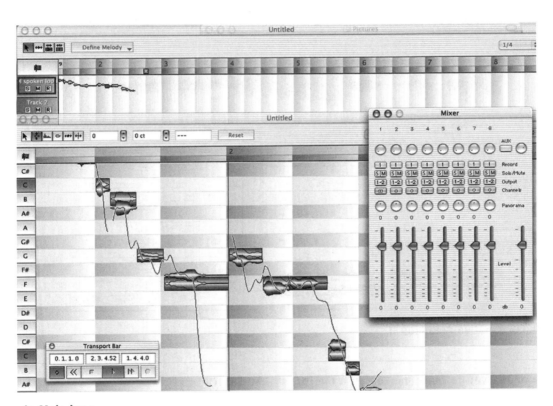

**Celemony's Melodyne**

When you load a file – a vocal recording, for example – into Melodyne and double-click the waveform, the program performs an analysis of the track. When this is complete, you then have a unique level of access to the material. Melodyne detects the melody underlying the audio material and divides the vocal recording up into syllables, which can be manipulated individually. Then, by manipulating the pitch, you can do things like change the tune; generate two-, three- or four-part

harmonies from copies of the same unison part; or impose the melody of one recording onto another. Melodyne also allows you to input audio and output MIDI that can be used to control a sampler or a synth.

And that's not all. Melodyne also enables you to move formants in a section of material in order to alter the timbre of individual syllables or even to change the tonal colour of an entire track – making a man's voice sound like a woman's, for example, and vice versa. Syllables can be stretched or shortened without their pitch being affected, the amount of vibrato can be increased or reduced and intonation or timing errors can be corrected without the phrasing ending up sounding unnatural. At the time of writing, there's no other program on the market that displays such an intelligent approach to audio analysis or offers the ability to modify audio data in such a musical way.

For more information on Celemony's products, visit www.celemony.com.

## Amadeus II

To give you an inkling of the type of software lurking in the shareware sector, here's a brief look at Amadeus II, a shareware application that runs native to Mac OS X. The program has been kept simple and pretty much frill-free, yet it offers all the basic functions you'd expect from a sample editor and a few more besides, such as support for files in MP3 and Ogg Vorbis formats, which it can open, edit and even save.

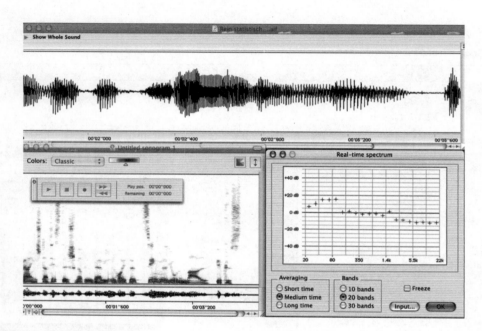

**HairerSoft's OS X-native Amadeus II**

Amadeus II allows you to place markers in a file to help with navigation, and it also comes with a variety of functions with which to analyse and repair audio recordings as well as a wide range of editing functions that can be supplemented with VST plug-ins.

Like all shareware programs, there's an imposed limit to Amadeus II's functionality. You're allowed to try it out free of charge for a 15-day period; after that, however, certain functions are deactivated, although these will be reactivated upon payment of a registration fee.

For more information about Hairersoft products, visit www.hairersoft.com.

## Audacity

Audacity actually takes the form of both a freeware sample editor and open-source software. It was originally developed by volunteers and is available on various platforms.

Audacity offers a limited number of functions (but all the most important ones) as well as a number of effects that can be applied to the audio files. It also enables you to load multiple audio files and play them back simultaneously, thus serving as a rudimentary audio sequencer. It's a nice program, and not just because it's free!

For more information, visit www.sourceforge.net.

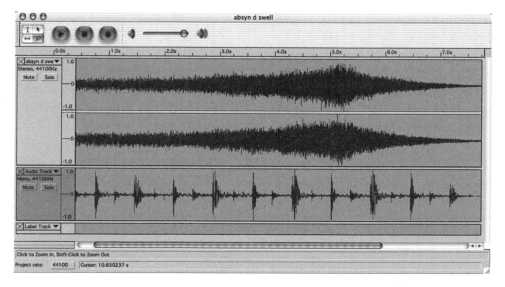

**Audacity, an open-source sample editor**

## CD Burning Software

When you're making music on the Mac, you need to be able to store and archive externally the various types of data you work with or you'll soon run out of hard-disk space, and probably a great deal sooner than you expected. The principal culprits when it comes to taking up disk space are usually audio samples taken from sound libraries that you access almost constantly, such as drum loops, single drum samples, pads, atmospheres and the like. These collections have a tendency to grow alarmingly and consume vast amounts of space, as samples are stored in AIFF or WAV format and are therefore uncompressed; for example, a single drum loop lasting only a few seconds could easily take up more space on your hard disk than a three-minute song in MP3 format – and, of course, you won't just want one drum loop on your hard disk but probably scores of them.

And that's not the only problem. When you're working with audio programs, you're constantly creating new audio files – a new file with each take, for example, and each time you render a track – and these, too, can quickly add up to a storage nightmare. And then, when recording is finished and you begin mastering, you're likely to want to keep various different arrangements or masters of the same project, which can also take up a lot of disk space.

In short, from time to time you're going to need to back up all non-essential data to another storage medium, and one of the best ways of doing this is to burn a CD. Blank CDs are cheap, comparatively robust and easy to archive, and all modern Macs come with an integrated CD burner, with the more expensive models equipped with a DVD burner, too.

It's easy to store all kinds of data on CD using the Finder. To set this up, go to the CDs & DVDs panel in the System Preferences, and where it says 'When you insert a blank CD', click the drop-down menu and select 'Open Finder'. Now, when you insert a blank CD, the Finder will place a blank CD icon on the desktop and you can then copy files to it and organise the data within it as easily as if it was a folder on your hard disk.

You can then burn the data to your CD. This is a once-only process (unless you're using CD-RW [rewritable] disks, which can be erased and used time after time), but it doesn't take place immediately; first the Finder creates an image of the CD to be burned on the hard disk, and at this point you can add, delete and reorganise files in the archive until you finally give the order to burn the CD.

However, there are two snags to using the Finder to burn your CDs. Firstly, the Finder always creates a 650MB image, even though you might have inserted a 700MB blank. Secondly, you need to have 900MB free on your hard disk – 650MB for the image plus the 250MB that OS X always needs in order to function. For this reason, you need to begin offloading data before you get down to your last 900MB of free space – unless, of course, you invest in a CD-burning program that uses a different system. Here are a few examples.

## Toast

Roxio's Toast is a program dedicated to burning CDs and DVDs – although of course you can only burn the latter if your Mac has a SuperDrive.

Toast scores over Mac OS X's own CD-writing solution in three important respects:

1  Toast recognises the capacities of the blank CD and behaves accordingly, whereas the Mac OS X Finder treats all blank CDs as having a maximum capacity of 650MB;

2  Toast can create CDs that can be read by a PC as well as a Mac, which makes it a lot easier to exchange data between the two machines;

3  Unlike the OS X Finder, Toast doesn't require you to have 900MB of free space on your hard disk because it doesn't create a disk image prior to burning the CD but simply copies the data directly from its original location to the CD.

As well as data CDs, Toast can be used to create audio CDs, although these days this isn't much of a selling point as Mac OS X already provides an elegant solution for this task in the form of iTunes.

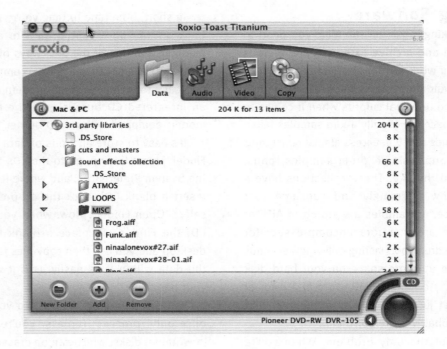

**Roxio Toast**

For more information about Roxio products, visit www.roxio.com.

## iTunes

Included free with every new Macintosh, iTunes's main task is to manage a computer-based music library, normally consisting of files in MP3 format. iTunes is capable of extracting (ie ripping) all the tracks from an audio CD, converting them to MP3 format and storing them on your hard disk, giving you a database from which to create your own playlists and write new CDs.

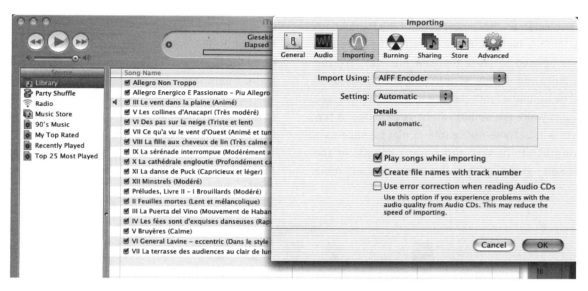

**Apple iTunes. Select 'AIFF Encoder' on the Preferences Import page to store ripped files in sequencer-friendly AIFF format on your hard disk**

iTunes can actually store files in AIFF or WAV format just as easily as it can MP3, whether you're ripping or burning to and from the hard disk. To rip files in AIFF format, simply alter the format on the Import page in the Preferences.

iTunes is a useful tool not only for those who like to listen to music but also for those who produce it for a living. Not only can it be used to rip CD tracks to the hard disk but also for the management of a sample library, whereby individual tracks can be classified using tags indicating artist, title, album, etc. If the 'Keep iTunes Music folder organised' box is checked on the Advanced page in the Preferences, iTunes will auto-name the folders in accordance with your tags as well and store the files in the correct folders.

## MP3 Conversion Software

Unlike AIFF and WAV formats, the compressed MP3 format has almost no role in computer-based music production. Although to many people the difference between MP3 and uncompressed audio is indiscernible, certainly at higher data rates, the fact is that in music production only a chronic shortage of free disk space would induce anyone to switch from using AIFF or WAV files to MP3s, even though the former require between eight and ten times as much storage space.

Nonetheless, the MP3 format remains highly useful, particularly for exchanging music files or samples via the Internet. Suppose, for example, you're collaborating with someone online – you're writing a song together, perhaps, or you want him to judge which is the better of two guitar solos. In such a case, you just need to convert the material to MP3 format, upload it and leave him to download the file, convert it back into AIFF or WAV format and then import it into his sequencer. At higher resolutions – certainly at 192KBps, and perhaps even lower – the difference between MP3 and the uncompressed audio is practically imperceptible.

### iTunes

As I mentioned earlier, iTunes can handle AIFF, WAV and MP3 formats. Usually you'll be using MP3 to store compressed copies of your CD library on the hard disk, but you could instead burn a compressed copy of your stored AIFF or WAV files onto CD.

If your WAV or AIFF source files form part of your hard-disk library, simply go to the iTunes window and select the files you want to convert, then Ctrl-click to call up a context menu and select 'Convert Selection to MP3' (as long as that option has been selected in the Preferences). The conversion is performed at the bit rate selected on the Import page of the Preferences dialog, and the higher the rate selected, the more disk space is needed to store the new file, but also the higher the audio quality. At 128KBps, the compressed file will be around a tenth the size of the uncompressed audio, but while the sound will be reasonable, a few artefacts will become noticeable in places, such as a smearing of the hi-hats and other cymbals. At the default setting of 160KBps, the loss in data is more

difficult to detect yet you'll still be saving a considerable amount of disk space. However, if you're planning on using the file for audio production, you should use the highest data rate, 192KBps.

iTunes also enables you to convert MP3 files back to AIFF or WAV format simply by changing the 'Import Using' setting on the Preferences Import page from 'MP3 Encoder' to 'AIFF Encoder' or 'WAV Encoder' and then selecting the files you wish to convert.

**Once you've selected 'MP3 Encoder', you can select the bit rate**

It might seem obvious but, if you convert a file from AIFF or WAV format to MP3 and then convert it back to the original format, the file you end up with won't be identical to the original file. This is because MP3 compression is what's known as *lossy* – ie some data is removed permanently. Even so, just because the two files aren't identical, it doesn't mean that anyone can tell the difference simply by listening to them; it really depends on how much information has been lost during the compression process, which in turn depends on the bit rate that was used during the initial conversion.

Regardless of the formats selected, the converted files will be stored in the same folder, which by default is the 'iTunes Music' folder in the 'Documents' folder of the user currently logged on. If you haven't used any tags to indicate the name of the artist or album, the folder will be named 'Unknown Artist' and the files will be stored in a sub-folder labelled 'Unknown Album'. Of course, if you have used the tags, both of these folders will be named something more appropriate.

## Notation Software

For those interested in turning out professional-looking scores, the score-writing functions of the top-of-the-line versions of Cubase and Logic are quite powerful. They're also more convenient than a specialist score-writing application, as all the data for the song in question will already be loaded into your sequencer.

However, if you're looking for something a little more flexible and powerful, you'll probably find it worthwhile to obtain a specialist notation program, and there are three currently available for Mac OS X: Sibelius 3 from the Sibelius group (www.sibelius.com), Finale 2004 (www.finalemusic.com) and Opus 1's NoteAbilityPro (http://debussy.music.ubc.ca/~opus1/), developed by Dr Keith Harnel. All three of these applications are also capable of outputting the data as MIDI messages – using the Apple DLS Music Device, for example – enabling you to double-check that what you've written does in fact sound the way you intended.

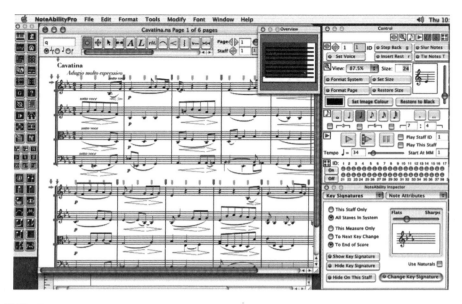

**Opus 1's NoteAbilityPro**

## Adding Sound To Video

It's also possible to add soundtracks to videos using the Mac. The sequencers Cubase and Logic and sample editors Spark and Peak will allow you to load and play back QuickTime movies in sync with your audio tracks.

Naturally, Apple's iMovie – free with every new Mac – can also perform this task. The music and sound effects themselves can be produced using any of the applications mentioned here as the audio data formats are compatible.

# 4  THE OPTIONAL EXTRAS

While, admittedly, it's possible to make music on the Macintosh with no accessories whatsoever, I can see no earthly reason for doing so, except simply to prove that it can, in fact, be done. It's much quicker to enter notes using a keyboard, or a drum loop using drum pads, than it is to perform either of these tasks using just the mouse.

For this reason, sooner or later you're likely to obtain a MIDI-input device, such as a keyboard, and perhaps a MIDI interface to link the keyboard to the computer. You might also want to improve the audio quality of your recordings and playback with an optional audio interface, perhaps with a microphone and preamp or mixer for recording acoustic signals.

External hardware such as a MIDI keyboard or fader box provides a faster and more intuitive way of entering data

You don't need a large number of external devices to produce music with the Mac. You could, of course, invest in an entire studio for it, complete with recording and control rooms, monitoring equipment, a mixer, effects devices and synths, but you can achieve perfectly satisfactory results at a fraction of the cost. Indeed, from a purely technical point of view, these days there's no difference between a project and a professional studio; they use much the same software, often producing results of similar quality.

A real studio has to cater for the requirements of a variety of different artists and perhaps even genres. You don't. You have the luxury of being able to concentrate solely on your own needs, so buy only the things you really need, but choose well. Even with just a good microphone, a good preamp and high-quality converters, you can come very close to the sound of a professional studio.

The following chapter looks in detail at those accessories you might find yourself needing, beginning with MIDI interfaces and MIDI-input devices like keyboards and fader boxes before moving on to the various accessories involved in audio recording.

## Optional MIDI Hardware
### MIDI Interfaces

Almost all electrical musical instruments and a great number of studio devices are equipped with MIDI ports through which they can send or receive MIDI messages. Your MIDI keyboard, for example, communicates with your synth or sampler by means of MIDI messages transmitted via its MIDI Out socket, and your sample player or effects devices receive MIDI data via their own MIDI Ins.

The Mac, too, needs a MIDI interface in order to be able to exchange MIDI data with such devices. This usually takes the form of an external device connected to the Mac via its USB or, sometimes, its FireWire interface.

The cheapest solution is a MIDI interface with one input and one output (ie 1 x 1). Since a single MIDI lead is capable of transmitting up to 16 channels of MIDI data, up to 16 different sounds or instruments can be controlled from the Mac with nothing more elaborate than this. Of course, for the data to reach all 16 devices, they'd have to be linked in a daisy-chain configuration, whereby the MIDI Thru of the first device feeds the MIDI In of the second, the Thru socket of which feeds a third device, and so on. In this case, you'd need to buy additional leads but no extra hardware.

The Mac is capable of receiving up to 16 channels of MIDI data simultaneously via the one MIDI In. Unfortunately, if you want to combine MIDI inputs, a daisy-chain configuration like the one described above but with the data flowing in the opposite direction won't work, and nor will soldering the cables. MIDI signals are digital. You can't just combine them; they must be merged intelligently.

For this, you need a MIDI merger, which is a small device capable of combining MIDI messages from

**The MIDISport Uno is one of the smallest MIDI interfaces on the market, offering one MIDI In and one MIDI Out**

multiple sources to create a single MIDI stream. These devices tend to be rather costly, however, and a simpler solution is simply to buy a MIDI interface with as many inputs as you need. Suppose, for example, you wanted to input data from two MIDI devices – a keyboard, perhaps, and a small fader box to control the onscreen mixer or effects plug-ins – at the same time. In this case, you'd need an interface with two MIDI Ins. There are also MIDI mergers that have four (4 x 4) and even eight inputs and outputs (8 x 8) should you wish to record the performances of several band members at the same time.

**The larger MIDI interfaces offer eight MIDI inputs and outputs**

Fortunately, today there are more and more keyboards and other MIDI devices on the market offering an integrated MIDI interface and which can be connected directly to the computer via USB. These devices are generally 'plug and play', capable of deriving their power from USB, making them independent of separate power supplies and therefore ideal for use with laptops.

MIDI interfaces can be obtained from most music shops and range in price from around £40 for a simple (1 x 1) model to around £270 for an 8 x 8 device. Before you buy any MIDI interface, however, make sure that Core MIDI drivers exist for it so that you can use it under Mac OS X. Thankfully, these drivers exist for most current models.

## Keyboards And Tone Generators

The chances are that you'll want a keyboard of some variety in order to play the virtual instruments in the computer. In this case, you don't need a keyboard with its own sounds or even its own audio signals, for that matter; it's possible to obtain keyboards that generate nothing more than MIDI messages, with no tone-generation sections of their own.

Devices like hardware synths and digital pianos, on the other hand, are capable of generating both MIDI messages and audio signals. The tone-generation sections of such instruments can be connected to the virtual instruments in your computer simply by connecting their output to the Mac's audio input, whether this is the integrated interface or an audio interface linked to the USB or FireWire port. The same thing goes for hardware tone generators without keyboards, such as rack modules or desktop samplers; they can be controlled via MIDI or, as is more common these days, via the USB port by a MIDI keyboard connected to the computer.

MIDI keyboards come in many shapes and sizes, the smallest having a range of only two octaves and intended primarily for performing live electronic sounds. For those of a more pianistic bent, however, there are larger models with 88-note hammer-action keyboards whose designers have gone to great lengths to recreate the feel of a grand piano.

Between these two extremes, there is an enormous number of models boasting keyboards of various lengths and with different features, such as the number and type of playing aids, control elements and pedal connections. If you're particularly interested in the action of the keyboard, you should visit your local music dealer and try out a few models. MIDI keyboards are also often equipped with knobs and faders – ideally, freely assignable ones – and these can be very useful for controlling software instruments, mixers or effects devices.

As I said earlier, keyboards that connect via USB are particularly convenient as you can invariably use them without a MIDI interface or separate power supply. Again, however, make sure that the keyboard is supplied with a Core MIDI driver for Mac OS X before you buy it.

**Novation's ReMOTE 25 is a MIDI keyboard with a generous supply of knobs and faders**

## Fader Boxes

It's a lot easier to use things like software tone generators, effects plug-ins and, of course, onscreen mixers if you have real knobs or faders to play with rather than onscreen controls. For one thing, with a hardware controller you can balance a pair of channels using both hands together, whereas with the mouse you have to adjust first one and then the other.

There are various types of fader boxes and controllers on the market that allow you to program the parameters of software effects devices and instruments remotely using MIDI messages, and virtually all music programs are compatible with these kinds of devices. Some controllers are modelled on mixing consoles, whereas others are nothing more than

**Ozone's compact M-Audio keyboard integrates both MIDI and stereo audio interfaces, making it ideal for use in the home studio and on the move**

COURTESY OF DOEPFER

**Doepfer's Pocket Fader, a classic fader box with 16 faders**

keyboards with a few knobs and faders thrown in. Increasingly, however, the tendency is for MIDI keyboards to be so well equipped with faders and data-entry devices of all kinds that they have both bases pretty well covered.

Rotary controllers come in two varieties, *absolute-value encoders* and *incremental encoders*, and before you buy a fader box you'll need to make sure that it has the right kind of encoders for the software you want to control with it. Absolute-value encoders are almost universally common (think of the knobs on your hi-fi or TV) and transmit absolute values for a parameter, whereas incremental encoders merely transmit messages to increase or decrease the current value by a certain amount. You generally can't spin the control of an absolute-value encoder through more than 360° (on your hi-fi, for example, you can turn the Treble control all the way up or down, but that's all), whereas an incremental encoder (sometimes described as a *data-entry wheel*) can be rotated freely in either direction as many times as you like. Of course, once you've reached the maximum or minimum value for the parameter the wheel is controlling, any further rotation is ignored.

So what's the point of an incremental encoder? Well, on your hi-fi, for instance, the only factor controlling the gain of the amplifier is the setting of the volume knob, so you can determine whether or not the volume is at its maximum level just by looking at the knob. In other words, the knob is like a clock that always tells the right time.

However, this isn't always the case with the knobs

of an incremental encoder, because they don't exercise continuous control over the parameters they're assigned to; they only send a message when you turn them. Also, the control they exert isn't exclusive, so if a parameter is set once using a hardware controller and this value is later changed using the mouse, the knob's position becomes both irrelevant and misleading.

Under these conditions, it's impossible to make subtle adjustments with an absolute encoder, but with an incremental encoder, it's easy. By rotating the knob a few degrees in either direction, the value is increased or reduced by a small amount, just as you'd expect. With an absolute encoder, however, as soon as you touch the knob, it transmits its current position, which might be a long way from its current *value*, and you might get a nasty jolt when the value jumps unexpectedly and you can't get the old setting back.

Even so, incremental encoders are inferior to absolute encoders in one (rather trivial) respect: they give you no visual feedback as to the current setting. Instead, you need to look at the computer monitor. An absolute encoder, on the other hand, tells you exactly what the current setting is, even though this might be a totally false indication of its current value.

As you move the hardware faders or knobs, MIDI controller data is sent to the software to control parameters such as volume and pan position. Under the MIDI standard, the data consists of a controller number (0–127) and a value in the same range (0–127). With a primitive fader box, a given fader will always transmit the same controller number, which means that, unless the software is particularly flexible, it can only ever be used to control a single parameter.

Provided that the software and the hardware controller assignments are in sync, everything should work fine – fader 1 will control the level of channel 1, fader 2 that of channel 2, and so on. However, if they're mismatched in any way, and neither is flexible, you could end up with a complete mess on your hands. For this reason, fader boxes generally allow you to determine which controller number will be assigned to each fader and knob on the device. The more sophisticated controllers even allow you to store entire setups so you can use one set of assignments to control the mixer and switch easily to a different set of assignments for your synth or an effects plug-in.

### Other Types Of Controller

Keyboard instruments aren't the only type of controller capable of generating MIDI note data. As well as drum pads, there are now MIDI-capable guitars, marimbas, brass instruments and accordions. Whatever your instrument of choice, there's a fair chance that a MIDI version of it exists and you'll be able to use it to input melodies, rhythms and perhaps even chords into a sequencer or even to control a virtual instrument.

As well as adapting conventional instruments to generate MIDI messages, today's developers have experimented with sensors of various kinds to create totally new forms of controller. M-Audio's Surface One, for example, utilises a fibre-optic-based touch-sensitive smart fabric to transduce the direction and pressure of each touch into a MIDI message, or even several messages simultaneously. However, it doesn't have to be touch; depending on the type of sensor, any type of movement could be used to generate MIDI messages – gestures, breath, etc. If you want to design a new type of sensor yourself, you'll probably find that you can purchase the electronic components you need over the Internet. The Doepfer site (www.doepfer.de) is always a good place to look.

There's a large number of manufacturers currently producing MIDI keyboards and fader boxes, including

**M-Audio's Surface One has touch-sensitive surfaces as well as incremental encoders**

Fatar (www.studiologic.net), Edirol (www.edirol.de), Evolution (www.evolution.co.uk), M-Audio (m-audio.com) and Doepfer (www.doepfer.de).

## Audio Recording Equipment

You might find that you'll never need to input audio signals to the computer. If all your source material is taken from sample CDs or else produced by soft synths inside the computer itself and mixed internally, you won't need audio inputs, just an output by which you can monitor the signal. However, if you're using external tone generators, such as hardware samplers or synths, or you want to record acoustic signals, an audio input of some kind is essential.

### Line In

In the simplest case, all you'll want to do is record the audio signal of some external device like a synth. Most have line-level stereo outputs like those of CD players, tape decks and DAT or MiniDisc recorders, so all you'll need is a cable with mini jacks on one end (for the computer) and whatever connectors the synth uses (probably normal-sized jacks) on the other. You should then – hardware permitting – be in a position to record the synth's stereo signal. The only other thing you might need to do is switch from 'Integrated Microphone' to 'Line In' on the Input page in the Sound panel of the System Preferences, but that should be it.

Aside from the fact that using integrated audio hardware is unlikely to produce the highest quality audio, the main potential problem with using it is that of latency. If there's too great a delay between pressing the key and hearing the note, this can make it virtually impossible to play rhythmically, let alone with any degree of sensitivity.

However, latency is no problem if you're only using an external tone generator to play back pre-recorded MIDI tracks. If the synth's signal is slightly behind that of the audio tracks, simply shift the data of the MIDI track controlling the synth a few milliseconds to the left.

If you're going to be inputting audio first from one device and then from another, and you don't own a mixer, you'll need to invest in a patchbay. Otherwise the action of connecting and disconnecting sockets to you Mac's audio input will weaken the socket. You'll also be sparing yourself a good deal of effort!

## Mic In

In order to record a vocal line or an acoustic instrument, you'll need a microphone, and since the signal from a microphone is far too weak for a line-level input, you'll need a preamp as well.

While your Mac's own audio hardware might offer a mic preamp, it's not designed for professional applications, and if you try to use it as such you're likely to end up with a recording containing a lot of artefacts – noise, distortion, hum, crackling, whistling, etc. For this reason, you're better off using an external mic preamp to bring the signal up to line level before it enters the computer. Even so, you might not need to go out and buy a preamp; you might find that your DAT, MiniDisc or cassette recorder already has one that you can insert into the signal chain between the mic and the computer's line in. Working this way is likely

to produce considerably better results than using the Mac's integrated hardware. And if you buy a high-quality audio card designed for music production, the chances are that it won't offer a mic preamp at all but will simply assume that you'll be using an external one.

## Channel Strips

The range of mic preamps on the market runs from rudimentary and very cheap devices to expensive channel strips resembling those found in fully featured mixing consoles and combining the functions of preamp, compressor, equaliser, de-esser and noise gate/expander. These latter kinds of devices might also feature valve (ie tube) technology, the characteristic distortion of which adds a certain warmth to the signal.

If you have an audio card with a digital stereo input (usually S/PDIF, optical or coaxial), it will probably contain a high-quality analogue-to-digital converter, allowing you to bypass the converters inside the computer.

**Channel strips like MindPrint's En-Voice combine the functions of a number of devices**

Remember, though, that any combination of mic, preamp or channel strip and audio card is only as strong as its weakest link; there's no point buying a channel strip with a digital output if the only signals it processes are those from third-rate microphones. Conversely, the considerable amount of money a first-class mic costs will be wasted if you're forced to rely on the Mac's own audio input.

## Mixing Consoles

While they're useful, channel strips are generally capable of processing only mono signals, so you might find that buying a small mixing console with integrated mic preamps will give you more flexibility when it

comes to feeding line-level audio into your computer. This is a fairly cost-effective solution and will save you a great deal of patching and unpatching of cables. The mixer's stereo output can be connected to the stereo input of the computer, thus removing the need for an audio card with multiple inputs.

If you want to feed your computer output to the mixer for monitoring purposes, you'll need to find a way of doing this while keeping it separate from the signal sent from the mixer to the computer input, or you'll set up a feedback loop. One way of doing this is by connecting the computer input to a pair of effects sends rather than the computer's main output buss, reserving the mixer's main output buss for monitoring

**A small mixer like Soundcraft's Spirit Notepad can make it easier to record external signals**

the computer output. A more practical (though more expensive) solution is to use a mixer with two sums, whereby one buss can be used to feed the computer's inputs and the other the studio monitors. Obviously, if you're using a digital mixer and your audio card offers both analogue and digital inputs, you should always opt for digital or you'll be converting the signal from digital to analogue and back again twice instead of only once.

Note that, even though in this case you're putting a hardware mixer between the computer and the monitors, you're not actually using it for mixing; in this setup, this function is performed by the sequencer's own mixer. Also, the resulting mix is already in stereo and shouldn't need any further treatment, so the hardware mixer's responsibilities are therefore pretty limited, its main task being to take the multiple input signals and create a single stereo output to feed the computer. You can also use it to provide the performers with a latency-free monitor mix instead of the one that's output by the computer.

## Multichannel Audio

The more audio signals you want to use in the virtual mixing and recording process, the more it makes sense to use audio hardware with multiple inputs and/or outputs rather than just a stereo pair at each end. Multichannel audio solutions generally take one of two forms: either they have multiple audio inputs and a stereo output, or they have multiple audio outputs and

a stereo input, although cards with multiple inputs and outputs do exist.

The first type of card – that with multiple audio inputs and a stereo output – is useful when it comes to recording live bands, as a separate input on the audio card can be assigned to each voice and main instrument, while the stereo output can be used to provide the foldback mix (ie the mix the band members listen to as they perform).

Meanwhile, the second type of card – that with multiple audio outputs and a stereo input – is used to create surround mixes. Here it's assumed that you're recording each instrument in turn (using the stereo input) and then either outputting a surround mix, or as many discrete signals as possible, to a hardware mixer. The most flexible solution is to use a card with multiple inputs and outputs, if you can afford one.

If you have a card with multiple inputs and you're using one or more external synths or samplers to play back one or more of your MIDI tracks, you have the luxury of being able to include these signals in the main mix before you've actually recorded them (in audio, as opposed to MIDI form). This leaves you free to go on changing MIDI notes and synth parameters right up until the last moment, when you're ready to begin mastering the track.

Of course, whether you still need a hardware mixer when you have a card like this depends on personal preference and how you work. However, if you dispense with the mixer and take the foldback mix from the computer, you'll inevitably suffer from a certain degree of latency.

## Digital Mixing Consoles

Many multichannel audio cards dispense with analogue inputs altogether, often offering digital interfaces in a format such as ADAT. This lets you combine any type of audio-to-digital converter with any type of card, or even to dispense with A/D converters altogether when working with digital devices. In such cases, a digital mixing console with outputs in ADAT format can prove very useful as it will allow you to feed 8, 16 or 24-plus digital audio channels simultaneously from the desk to the computer or vice versa.

Of course, it's impossible to say whether or not a

digital mixer is better than an analogue one for routing signals to a computer, or better than the sequencer's virtual mixer at mixing down, as this kind of judgement is likely to depend on personal taste, working habits and the nature of the material. The hardware mixer's specifications and the software's stock of plug-ins are also contributing factors.

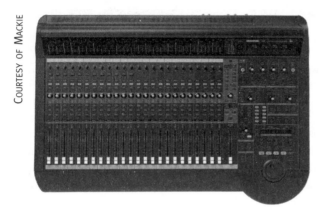

**Mackie's d8b is a medium-sized digital mixer**

For the highest possible degree of automation, you're probably better off using the integrated onscreen mixer, as it's normally impossible to store the settings of the analogue gain controllers using a (hardware) digital mixer.

## Optional Audio Hardware

I've said it before, but it's worth repeating: as a musician, you should look on the specs for most home computers' integrated audio hardware with a good deal of scepticism. Aside from the G5, with its digital interfaces, Apple computers are no exception here, although the audio outputs of the G4 are high-spec enough for many purposes.

The main problem is with the input. Some Macs, including the iBook range and even some Power Books, have no audio inputs at all, while those supplied with other models are seldom suitable for serious professional recording, tending to be far too noisy.

Then there are limitations on the number of channels you can use simultaneously. The Mac's integrated audio hardware offers just a stereo input and stereo output – obviously inadequate for a surround production or for recording an entire band.

In either case, the solution is to invest in additional audio hardware, and this next section gives a brief overview of the types of hardware currently available. You'll need to decide at the outset whether or not you want the audio hardware to be capable of handling mic-level signals or only line-level ones; in the latter case, if you do ever want to record using a microphone, you're going to need to insert a mixer with mic inputs or a separate mic preamp into the signal chain.

### PCI Audio Cards

The best solution for desktop computers is still to use audio cards for the PCI buss. There are currently a number of makes and models on the market offering a variety of solutions, such as those with more inputs than outputs (or vice versa), those with connectors mounted in breakout boxes, cable whips or on the base-plate at the back of the computer, and those with or without MIDI ports.

Audio cards often offer digital connectivity in one or more of the standard formats, such as dual-channel S/PDIF or eight-channel ADAT interfaces. By dispensing with onboard analogue connectors and offering multiple ADAT interfaces, these kinds of cards are capable of inputting and outputting dozens of digital audio channels simultaneously. They also often employ external breakout boxes, often in rack format, with integrated analogue-to-digital converters in order to accommodate analogue signals, too. The ADAT

**M-Audio's Delta 1010LT is a multichannel audio card for the PCI buss with a cable whip**

interface, which has become a popular standard for such cards, makes it possible to combine the cards and converter units of different manufacturers.

If you're running a large studio equipped with powerful desktop Macs and you need to input multiple channels simultaneously, you might want to invest in a multichannel digital PCI card. For those with more modest needs – a handful of external devices at most, for example – a more cost-effective solution would be to buy one of the USB or FireWire solutions discussed below.

PCI audio cards with Mac OS X drivers are manufactured by RME (www.rme-audio.com), MOTU (www.motu.com) and M-Audio (www.m-audio.com), among others.

## USB And FireWire Audio Interfaces

USB and FireWire interfaces have an advantage over PCI cards in that you just have to plug them in. Not only does this save you the trouble of having to fiddle around with a screwdriver and opening up the computer, but it also allows you to use the same interface on different computers (although not, obviously, at the same time). Of course, iMacs and laptops don't actually have PCI slots, which makes the choice somewhat simpler!

The bandwidth of the USB 1 standard allows for the transmission of around eight audio channels simultaneously. Most of the solutions based on this standard offer either two inputs and two outputs, or two inputs and six outputs (for surround), or four of each, although you sometime come across other permutations. These interfaces vary in size from ultra-compact stereo-cable-format models to multichannel line models and devices with integrated preamps. Many of them are plug and play and so don't require separate power supplies.

USB audio interfaces are now available from many manufacturers, including Emagic (www.emagic.de), which produces two EMI models: one with two inputs and six outputs and the other with six inputs and two outputs. Other USB and FireWire interfaces are produced by Egosys (www.esi-pro.com), M-Audio (www.m-audio.de) and Edirol (www.edirol.de).

There are currently fewer audio interfaces that make

**Manufacturer ESI offers a variety of FireWire audio interfaces**

use of the FireWire protocol, although that might be about to change. The FireWire standard stipulates for the exchange of data at 32 times the speed of USB 1 (ie 400MBps). At these kinds of speeds, USB 2 and FireWire are roughly equivalent.

Mark Of The Unicorn (www.motu.com) has already established a good reputation in this field, its 828 eight-channel FireWire audio interface being ideal for home recording, while Presonus's mLAN-based FireStation is somewhat similar (www.presonus.com). M-Audio's FireWire 410 is a mobile plug-and-play device with four inputs and ten outputs (www.m-audio.de), while Egosys's (www.esi-pro.com) QuataFire 610 is a six-in/ten-out 24-bit, 96/192kHz mobile recording interface using the FireWire port.

The mLAN alliance, with currently around 100 manufacturer members, can be expected to weigh in very soon with interfaces based on the Yamaha standard, which is designed to allow easy networking of multiple devices, with all audio and MIDI data transmitted by a common FireWire cable. Indeed, Yamaha recently launched the mLAN-based 01X, an attractive and economical combination of a digital mixer and software interface, as well as the i88x, a 24-bit/96kHz audio interface featuring two instrument/mic phantom-powered inputs, six line inputs, ADAT I/O, S/PDIF I/O and MIDI I/O. mLAN drivers for Mac OS X are currently under development.

For more information about the mLAN alliance, check out www.yamahasynth.com/pro/mlan/index.html.

## PC Audio Cards

PC cards are to certain laptops what PCI cards are to desktops. In the Mac range, both of the larger Power Books are equipped with PC card slots, whereas the iBooks and 12" Power Book don't have them.

In the audio sector, there are very few solutions in PC card format, and with the advent of USB and FireWire their number is unlikely to grow. Nonetheless there are one or two high-quality audio interfaces available for Mac OS X in PC card format, notably the two- and four-channel VXpocket v2 cards developed by French manufacturer Digigram (www.digigram.com) and RME's (www.reme-audio.de) multichannel Hammerfall DSP system.

# 5  PRACTICALITIES

This chapter looks at the tasks involved in creating computer-based music and the order in which they're normally performed – in most cases, by one and the same person.

When it comes to making music, different people have different goals and ways of working, and consequently different approaches, priorities, preferred applications and workflow. With this in mind, this chapter includes a number of techniques that have proved their value over the years, along with a few suggestions to guide you through the maze of possible approaches. Since at some point you're bound to come face to face with an onscreen mixer, regardless of how you work, the subject of mixing is dealt with later in this chapter.

Your working methods have a direct bearing on how much processing power you need. People often overload their computer's CPU unnecessarily either through failing to understand the software they're working with or without thinking clearly about what they're trying to do. There's a section at the end of this chapter that examines this problem in greater detail and explores ways of making more efficient use of the processing power you have available so you don't automatically reach for your chequebook every time something goes wrong.

Finally, there's a brief look at some of the ways your Mac can help you in live performance.

## How Music Is Produced
### Composition
Of all the activities involved in music production, composition is the one over which the computer has the least influence. Creating beautiful harmonies, dreaming up catchy melodies and devising grooves that make people want to get up and dance have more to do with inspiration, ingenuity and concentration than with hardware, software or a secure power supply.

Inspiration comes to different people at different times; some have their best ideas in the shower, others while they're out jogging, others while tinkering about at the keyboard. And then there are those people who seem to find their inspiration by looking at the charts and seeing what's selling...

If you're one of those people who have their best ideas at the most inconvenient moments, you might want to try carrying a dictaphone or a portable phone around with you, or perhaps a palmtop with a record function. Then, if a good tune comes to you in the supermarket or in the car, you can make a note of it before you have time to forget it.

Much the same applies when you're improvising at the keyboard. As soon as you have an idea, even though it might not be fully developed, record it as quickly as possible. Otherwise, the phone will ring and the idea will be lost forever.

To compose music for a conventional instrument, such as the piano, not only do you need to be able to play it, but you also need to know enough about notation to capture your ideas on the page before they fade from your memory. But what if you love music but have no musical training? If you buy a computer, can you dispense with music lessons altogether, or doesn't it work like that?

The answer is: it depends. The computer is an extremely powerful tool, but it can't do your thinking for you. If you want to write in the style of a Classical or Baroque composer, you need to be able to *think* like one, which involves acquiring the same set of mental skills; whether you learn from books or take a course in composition, you'll essentially be following the same path, beginning mastering simple forms and then learning to combine them in increasingly complex and original ways. Of course, with some modern genres, such as techno, you need to learn a different set of skills revolving around knowing how to use the hardware and software in your recording environment.

However, there's a lot more to modern music and computer-based music production than just arranging notes; the traditional rules of composition and playing technique still have a role to play (albeit a less prominent one) in most modern genres, and yet in others they're completely redundant. Meanwhile, synths, samplers and computers have opened up new fields of musical expression, and without some kind of skill in using these you'll be no better off than 10,000 other people with the same dream. However, the skills you choose to take with you on your musical journey and those you regard as useless baggage will depend on the direction you're planning to take and how far you're willing to go.

## Collage

Arranging loops, phrases and textures derived from sample CDs and CD-ROMs in a musically meaningful manner is more a form of collage than composition in the conventional sense. But this doesn't mean that it's in any way inferior; it's a new approach to music-making, inspired and made possible by the computer, and the quality and character of the end result might be indistinguishable from that of music produced in the traditional way.

You don't need to be able to play an instrument to make music with a computer; it's perfectly possible to enter the notes using the mouse or the computer keyboard. And if you do use a traditional (ie piano-style) keyboard but make a mess of the performance, you can always correct the mistakes and clean up the timing on the computer at the editing stage. If you want to share your ideas with other performers, you don't even need to know anything about notation or the names of the chords; the best software takes dictation – you play, it writes it down. And as for harmony, you can rely on trial and error. What you *do* need, however,

is a feeling for music and a good ear. Passion, determination and the occasional spark of inspiration won't hurt, either.

This isn't to imply that a traditional musical education has no value in the computer age; it has the same value it always had, and the more skill you have, whether as composer or as player, the larger the universe of possibilities you can explore. Having said that, it's true that sometimes a musical education proves counter-productive, stifling the imagination and instilling a reluctant to explore new avenues.

## Recording

As well as being a compositional tool and an electronic tone generator, the computer can also be the central unit in a recording studio, if need be. The recording of audio is no longer an essential part of music production; drum machines are often used in place of real drum sets, while what sounds like a guitar or a piano is often in fact a synth. Even vocals can be derived from sample CDs, transformed perhaps beyond recognition using audio-editing software.

With the right software and a little additional hardware, the Mac can supply the same functionality as a recording studio in all the most important respects. However, a word of warning: No amount of equipment is going to give your broom cupboard the acoustics of a good recording room, nor will your bedroom ever be as comfortable to produce music in as the control room of a well-designed studio.

Then, of course, there's the matter of expertise. The reputations of the great recording studios are built partly on the skill and experience of the recording engineers that work in them. It isn't enough to have the right microphones; you need to know which ones to use, when to use them and where to place them, and much the same applies to all the other equipment in the studio. Although with a Mac running the right software, and with the right hardware accessories, its possible to come very close to the sound of a good studio, this doesn't mean you'll automatically be able to achieve the same results as the top commercial studios – at least, not right away.

In order to create really good recordings, you'll first need to upgrade from the Mac's integrated hardware.

With the exception of the Power Mac G5, which offers digital inputs and outputs, the audio inputs (if any) of the current range of Macs are fine if you're simply using the computer as a musical sketchpad, but they're not designed for the creation of high-quality acoustic recordings. For that you'll need a good audio interface plus a good microphone, a good mic preamp and perhaps even a small mixer.

Once you've decided to include acoustic recording in your music production, your recording studio becomes increasingly less virtual and some of the problems and expense of traditional recording start to apply. As demonstrated in the previous chapter, the range of hardware accessories is very wide, and while you can't embark on acoustic recording without spending some money, quite how much you need to spend depends on what it is you plan to record and what kind of audio quality you're aiming for. A microphone alone could set you back a few thousand pounds, and the best mic for your voice won't be the same as the best one for your drum kit or Spanish guitar.

Like I said, though, acoustic recording is optional. You can make good music using only software instruments and material derived from sample CDs, in which case the only additional accessories you'll need are a MIDI interface and a small keyboard with which to play software instruments.

## Arranging

In the context of sequencers, the word *arranging* refers to the fleshing out of musical ideas to create a finished work. This arranging takes place both vertically and horizontally. The vertical element might involve such things as generating three-part harmonies from a recording of a single voice, adding pads (mostly likely soft synth chords) to spell out the harmonies and sharing material between various instruments or synth patches. This vertical element, therefore, can be seen as combining harmonisation with orchestration.

The horizontal element, meanwhile, involves the sequential ordering of sections (intro, verse, chorus, etc), and this is performed in the sequencer's Arrange window using clipboard functions (Cut, Copy and Paste), just as you'd edit text in a word processor. This aspect of arranging is more concerned with structure and form.

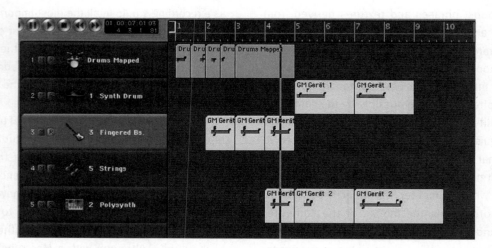

**Arranging MIDI recordings in a sequencer**

When you think of a tune, it's often the case that you think of the harmony at the same time. You might not know the name of a chord, but you'll very definitely recognise it when you hear it, and likewise you'll know that another chord is 'wrong' even though it might still fit with the melody. So even though I've described composing and arranging as being two different tasks, with adding harmonies to a melody being more the domain of arranging, when you harmonise a melody you're not really taking any bold new steps; you're not inventing; you're just discovering. With a little more experience, you'll find that, when you think of a tune in the bath, you'll know what chords should sound beneath it even before you've sat down at the piano or guitar to work them out.

The distinction between composing and arranging is therefore somewhat artificial. In classical music, for example, both tasks are performed by the same person, and usually at the same time. True, some classical composers wrote their symphonies in two stages, beginning with a piano version of each movement and then orchestrating it later, but even then the harmonies and melodies were written at the same time, with only the orchestration postponed to a later date.

The orchestration aspect of arranging offers more scope for creativity today than it did in the days of Beethoven or even Mahler. Classical composers could only combine the sounds of existing instruments to create new textures, whereas these days it's possible to actually create new sounds. This aspect of music production, known as *sound design*, is a totally new discipline. Each time you create a new sound, it's equivalent to creating a new instrument – something that Beethoven and Mahler never did (at least, as far as we know!). Of course, it might not make much difference; the song might sound just as good and sell just as well if the chords are played on a Fender Rhodes with a smidgen of chorus instead of using the synth patch you spent six hours programming. Nonetheless, the modern synthesiser's facility for creating totally new sounds adds a new dimension to musical expression, and good sound design can occasionally make a big difference.

Sometimes sound design takes place in a non-musical context. Someone was paid, for example, to program the factory presets for your synth. When you select one of these presets, or a particularly lush pad from a sample CD, and use it to fill in the background harmonies for a song chorus, you're essentially just orchestrating your composition. The only difference is that you have a wider palette, with electronic sounds as well as traditional ones at your disposal. However, if you're programming in your own sounds, you're making sound design part of the job of arranging.

Along with the form and texture of an arrangement, a key element is rhythm. Noise and ambient sounds – car horns, police whistles, breaking waves or conversation in a crowded bar – are also sometimes added to create atmosphere or a dramatic context, all of which comes under the general heading of arranging.

## Mixing

While the distinctions between composing, harmonisation and arranging might be artificial, it's much easier to look at mixing as being a separate task, and although in the home or project studio songwriters and bands might mix their own music, in professional studios the task of mixing is usually assigned to a specialist.

Whereas in classical-music composition harmonisation and arranging are all tasks performed by the same person (the composer), mixing is closer to the job of conducting. Like conducting, the art of mixing is partly about finding the correct balance between the various instruments in a mix. Of course, the tasks of both the conductor and the mix engineer go much further than this, and while the mix is designed to support the composer's objectives, most of the mix engineer's actions will be based on technical rather than musical considerations, and

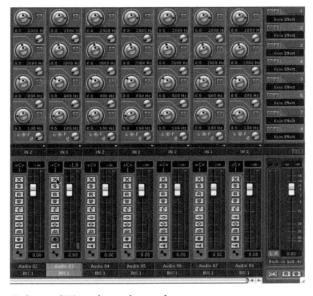

**Cubase SX's mixer channels**

these might be the same no matter what material he's mixing.

I should point out here that, although a MIDI-plus-audio sequencer's onscreen mixer might seem a poor substitute for the vast consoles you find in major recording studios, in terms of performance there's very little to choose between them.

## Volume

As I mentioned earlier, one of the principal tasks involved in mixing is finding a balance between the volume levels of the individual tracks. This doesn't mean that all the instruments should be as loud as each other, of course, but no instrument should be permitted to drown out the others and each should be given its own space in the sonic image.

## Tone

The second key task involved in mixing is correcting the frequency response of the individual signals, which is the job of the equaliser. But what's corrected, why is it corrected, and how is it done?

While each of the signals present in the input channels has frequency components that are characteristic of its sound and crucial to its profile within the mix, it also has others that are unnecessary and even counter-productive. With the acoustic guitar, for example, the mid-range and higher frequencies – which contain both the plucking sound and the characteristic timbre of the strings – are the ones you

want to keep, whereas the low mid-range and bass sounds – which play a less important role in defining the sound of the instrument – can safely be dispensed with, as all they're really doing is competing with other instruments and cluttering the sonic image. Therefore, to keep the mix as transparent as possible, the superfluous low-frequency components of the acoustic-guitar signal are heavily attenuated, leaving only those frequencies that are most characteristic of the instrument's sound. These can then be polished further, perhaps by boosting the higher frequencies slightly to add freshness and presence.

In mixing, each of the instruments is generally assigned its own band of frequencies, from which other instruments are excluded. At the same time, tonal imbalances – due perhaps to poor room acoustics or mic technique – are also corrected using the equaliser. For example, some instruments have a tendency to boom in parts of the lower mid range or suffer a dullness due to the loss of high frequencies.

In each case, the way each instrument sounds on its own is less important than how it sounds in the context of the mix, with all the other instruments playing. You might find that, when you solo a particular instrument, it sounds dreadful – too thin or top-heavy – but that doesn't mean the mix engineer has done a bad job. After all, each instrument is supposed to contribute something different to the mix, so it would be more surprising if they didn't sound unbalanced when heard on their own.

As you fine-tune the frequency response of each instrument (ie each channel), you're looking to treat the way it sounds with the other instruments, not on its own. The classic blunder made by beginners is to solo a channel ('so I can hear what I'm doing') before adjusting its EQ. This is a great way of getting the best possible sound for each instrument on its own, but that's missing the whole point of mixing; the whole, in this case, is not equal to the sum of its parts. It doesn't matter how the lead guitar sounds on its own because you never hear it on its own.

## Spatial Imaging

A good stereo recording creates the impression that each voice or instrument is coming from a separate

**Logic Platinum's eight-band channel equaliser**

and distinct point in space, somewhere between the left and right speakers, and this is known as its *spatial imaging*. The more distinct the impression, the better the spatial imaging – or, in mixer jargon, the better the localisability of the phantom image.

Ideally the listener should have a clear sense of both the distance and the direction of each sound source, in which case both the 'depth imaging' and the 'directional imaging' are said to be good. The directional imaging relies on a combination of three factors: differences in the volume, phase and frequency response with which the same source is reproduced in the two channels. For instance, if the violin sounds louder, brighter and a split second earlier in the right channel than the left, the listener will interpret it to be coming from the right. In other words, the phantom image will be somewhere to the right of centre.

The depth imaging, meanwhile, is an illusion based on the fact that the greater the distance between the listener and the sound source, the duller the sound, because the higher frequencies fall away more rapidly than the lower frequencies as a sound recedes into the distance.

In this context, it's worth bearing in mind that even in nature lower frequencies are harder to localise than higher ones, their phantom images being less distinct, to the extent that sounds like bass guitar and kick drum effectively have no phantom image at all. In this case, there's no point in panning them either to the right or to the left; you'd make better use of your available resources to have their energy load split between both speakers.

As I mentioned in the section about reverberation, the friction between air molecules robs high frequencies of energy at a faster rate than it does low frequencies, which explains why sounds arriving from a distance have a tendency to sound not only quieter but also duller than those originating nearby. Therefore, if you want to place a particular sound source at the rear of the sonic image – at the back of the orchestra, the rear of the stage, the back row of the choir, etc – you need to make it not only quieter but also duller by attenuating the higher frequencies. If it sounds too bright, the impression of distance will be lost.

Mixing is the best time to apply effects such as reverb, delay, chorus, flanging, compression and distortion. Reverb also contributes to the spatial impression, placing the sonic events in the context of a real room by simulating the early and late reflections from the walls, floor and ceiling. However, there are many reasons, both aesthetic and practical, why effects should be used.

## Mastering

The final part of the production process, the mastering stage involves optimising the sound quality and the overall volume level, adding fade-ins or -outs and matching the level of each track to those around it. Essentially, the idea is to adapt the music to the medium and use for which it is destined.

The mastering process gives you an opportunity to apply the final polish to the sound in order to obtain a sonic image that's rounded and balanced, while any errors introduced at the mixing stage can be removed, such as particular frequency ranges being boosted or attenuated. If you're putting together an album, for example, you need to make sure that neither the bass nor the treble stands out on one track more than another; you can't expect listeners to leap out of their armchairs to adjust the tone or volume every time a new track starts.

Although mastering is undoubtedly an important stage of music production, the less of it you have to do, the better. Similarly, the better the mix, the more straightforward the mastering. The greater danger is of doing too much. Nevertheless, certain things do have to be checked, such as how the material sounds on different types of playback system and in different environments, as well as whether or not it bears sustained listening; for example, the bass might sound fine on your studio monitors and yet make an awful booming noise on your car stereo, while a sound that's too bright can become tiresome after a while.

Also, in order to actually improving a recording at the mastering stage, you need good ears as well as a certain amount of experience. Listening carefully to the work of other producers can make it easier to detect the flaws in your own work.

In addition to refining the sound quality, the

mastering stage is where you need to optimise the overall volume level as well as the dynamic range. Compression is often applied to the main mix at this stage, with a view to making the sound more compact and powerful and to increase the impression of loudness. This is especially important if you want your material to sound good on the radio, as a loud and heavily compressed sound seems to go down better with listeners.

**Limiters, like this one from TC Works, allow you to increase the intensity of the main mix**

At the risk of stating the obvious, it's possible to apply too much dynamic processing, leaving it sounding flat, mushy and even oppressive. Less is often more when it comes to compression, but habit and listener expectation mean that it's usually best to apply some, at least.

Once you've applied the final bit of polish and all the necessary processing has been applied, the next stage is generally to normalise the mix – ie to bring it up to the maximum level consistent while avoiding distortion and bearing in mind the noise-control guidelines of radio stations. The idea is to take maximum advantage of the available audio resolution, as well as to ensure that the material sounds good and punchy.

It may also be necessary to top and tail the recording, making sure that the tracks start and end cleanly (if they don't fade out) and that there's no distracting hiss or breath noise before the first note. It's not too late to apply a fade-in or -out or a crossfade here and there before the tracks are finally written to the CD.

# Working With MIDI And Audio
## MIDI
The most common way of working with a MIDI-plus-audio sequencer dates back to the days when the computer could handle only MIDI, not audio, and therefore used external MIDI instruments. You connected your MIDI keyboard to the Mac and loaded the sequencing software, which was able to record whatever you played in much the same way that a word processor records whatever you type.

The procedure is essentially the same today, except that software instruments are used increasingly in place of external tone generators.

In the early stages of composition, most people put their sequencer into Loop or Cycle mode, whereby a song segment repeats endlessly while they try out different ideas.

The keyboard is connected to the MIDI In socket of the hardware interface and routed from within the computer either to the MIDI Out socket of the same interface or to a software tone generator loaded into the sequencer as a plug-in. On most sequencers, in order to select the destination of the MIDI messages recorded on each track, you normally first have to select the track and then the instrument from a pop-up menu listing all available tone generators, or their outputs or channels. Once each track's output has been selected, you can change instrument simply by selecting a different track.

Working this way, you can compose a song in segments, instrument by instrument or track by track (which is essentially the same thing). For example, you might begin with the drum track, adding first the kick drum, then the snare, then the hi-hat, toms and cymbals before switching to a second track and trying out a few bass-guitar lines, then switch to another track and lay down the harmonic foundation with a few chords on an electric-piano patch or a synth pad before moving on to add a trumpet, lead synth or whatever else takes your fancy. Working this way, you can build up complex rhythmic and melodic textures with no musical training whatsoever, and it's scarcely more difficult than whistling in the shower, because you can enter the parts one at a time – or even one note at a time – and build up the arrangement layer by layer.

Another reason why this way of working is so easy is that you can correct mistakes quickly and easily, even those you made back at the beginning of the piece. You can correct wrong notes in any of half a dozen different ways, such as clicking on a note and pressing the Up arrow on the computer keyboard as many times as necessary (moving it up a semitone each time), dragging it with the mouse or going back to the keyboard and playing the note you meant to play in the first place. If the note was too quiet, you can make it louder; if it sounded too soon, you can move it forwards or backwards in time; if it cuts off too early, you can stretch it to the correct length; if you think a phrase you played on the synth would sound better on the trumpet, you can select the notes with the mouse and drag them from the synth track to the trumpet track. You can also add modulation-wheel movements to a recorded track in order to add vibrato – again, correcting mistakes where necessary – and even tidy up the timing of an entire arrangement with a single mouse-click.

Once you're happy with the first part of your song, simply move the left and right markers (between which recording takes place) and start work on the next part, which could be the chorus, intro or coda – it really doesn't matter, as you can rearrange the parts in any order.

Finally, when you think you've got enough material to keep the listener interested for a few minutes (even though, without repeats, it might barely come to 20 seconds), you can copy and move the various sections to different points in the timeline (indicated by a ruler at the top of the screen showing the bar numbers) until you have a song with a structure – intro, verse, verse, chorus, verse, chorus, etc. Alternatively, if you're working in the techno genre, you might want to repeat your first loop 32 times, progressively thinning out the instruments by working backwards from bar 32 to the beginning so that, when the song plays back, you begin with just the drums and bass and the other instruments enter one by one. This can be done by muting all the tracks and then unmuting them one at a time at the right moments. As is almost invariably the case when you're working with a sequencer, if you aren't satisfied with the results, you can undo your actions with a click of the mouse.

You might find certain transitions too sudden, or certain passages too monotonous, in which case you can insert new material to even things up. If all you've recorded so far is the song accompaniment, at some point you'll need to record other parts such as vocals, guitar solo, acoustic-guitar accompaniment and other licks and fills from acoustic or other non-MIDI instruments, all of which are recorded via the audio interface, with or without a mic and preamp inserted into the signal chain.

At some point you'll also need to record the audio signals of any external MIDI-compatible synths and samplers you're using by connecting each device's audio output to the computer's audio input. As the track plays back, the MIDI messages are sent from the computer to the instrument, which responds by generating audio signals, which in turn are recorded by the sequencer in a new track. Thereafter, the MIDI track can be muted (or even deleted entirely) and the hardware instrument freed up to be used on another track.

Working this way, you can build up a full arrangement and mix piece by piece, adding effects to the tracks where necessary. At this stage, the entire production is generally rendered (or *bounced*) to the hard disk and the computer creates a single mono, stereo or surround audio file. It does this by performing all the same tasks as it did during playback – reading the right parts of the right audio files at the right time, generating audio signals from the software instruments, applying processing and implementing the pan and level settings, etc – and then writing the resulting audio file to disk. This audio file can then be loaded into a sample editor, in order to be compressed, mastered and written to CD, or else converted to MP3 format for Internet distribution.

Finally, the song document (also known variously as the *project* or *production*) containing the arrangement, along with all settings, automation data and constituent audio files, needs to be archived onto CD or DVD so that, if you ever decide you want to work on it again, you can simply load it back into the sequencer and take up where you left off.

This, at least, is one possible way of approaching music production on the Mac. Naturally, there are many others, especially as regards MIDI input, where you could use any means of inputting MIDI data – a MIDI drum

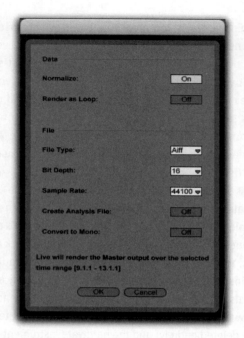

**Ableton Live's Render dialog, which determines the audio format, bit resolution and sampling frequency of the resulting audio file**

then move, copy or delete the various segments in the sequencer's sample editor or replace them with new takes. Admittedly, audio data isn't as malleable as MIDI, but in the sequencer it can be edited non-destructively, which is less nerve-racking than fiddling about with razor blades and splicing tape.

Even if you're working exclusively with audio, that doesn't mean you're restricted to working with recordings of acoustic instruments and vocal tracks; you could just as easily create a collage of material derived from sample CDs or the Internet. The world is literally full of sound, the musical uses of which are limited only by the imagination of the user.

When you're looking for a new sound or pattern, you might need to look no further than your own hard disk. As you work with music software, you'll no doubt be trying out new programs and instruments, harvesting new sounds as you come across them. Ideas that have no place in the project you're currently working on could easily be the inspiration for your next piece, so it's a good idea to make a note of ideas for songs or sounds as they

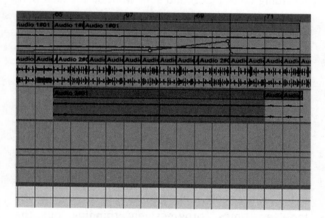

**Audio tracks in Ableton Live's Arrange view**

pad, for example – rather than a keyboard. Alternatively, you could dispense with a MIDI instrument altogether, choosing instead to enter notes manually with the computer keyboard and mouse or a step sequencer, a device widely used in genres such as techno as a practical means of generating repeating patterns.

However you choose to work, the basic principle remains the same. First you get some ideas down and record or program in the MIDI tracks. These are then edited and audio tracks are added. The data is then arrangement and mixed, and the entire project is then bounced to disk. In this way, MIDI becomes audio.

## Audio

All this talk about MIDI will perhaps be of no interest to those who play in purely acoustic bands or perform exclusively *a cappella*, and who can therefore dispense with MIDI altogether and use just audio tracks.

Working with audio tracks on the sequencer is something like working with an analogue multitrack tape recorder, except that the sequencer is far more flexible and can perform the same tasks very quickly. On a sequencer, you can even slice up audio data and

come to you. Many applications offer a 'Record to Disk' function whereby you can capture the computer's output signal and store it as an audio file on the hard disk.

In fact, the simplest solution is a freeware utility from Ambrosia Software (www.ambrosiasw.com) called WireTap, which allows you to record the current stereo output signal of the Mac to the hard disk at the touch of a key. This program's functions are available regardless of which application you're using at the time or the audio material's source. It makes no difference whether you want to record from your MP3 player, from an Internet radio station or from a software synth – all are handled just as easily and in the same way.

## Manipulating Audio Data

While audio tracks are easier to work with than magnetic tape, they're not as easy to manipulate in the sequencer as MIDI tracks, largely because the laws of physics dictate that the faster you play back an audio file, the higher the pitch, and if you slow down playback, the pitch drops. In this respect, an audio file on your computer is no different from tape.

However, recent developments in the audio sector allow you to adjust the pitch and playback speed of audio material independently of each other, and programs such as Ableton Live and Celemony Melodyne will allow you to perform such wizardry. (Check out Chapter 3, 'The Software', for more on these programs.)

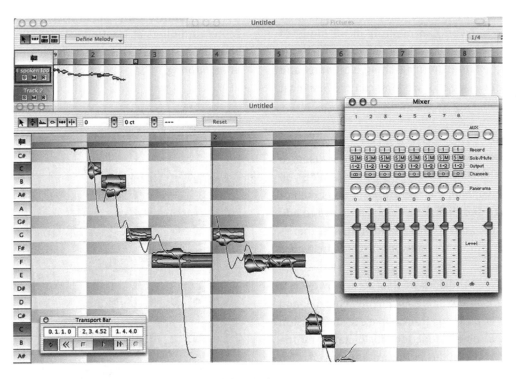

**In Melodyne, out-of-tune notes can be corrected in pitch as well as lengthened or shortened**

Although the two applications are different in terms of their design concept, as well as in the type of results that they produce, both allow a far more fluid approach to the manipulation of audio data than conventional audio sequencers. While they offer fewer conventional editing functions and effects as sequencers, and MIDI tracks have been dispensed with altogether, they're valuable additions to your music toolbox, especially if you're interested in experimenting with audio material.

## Mix And Match

There are still other ways of making music on the Mac. As I mentioned in Chapter 3, it's possible to produce music using nothing more than Propellerhead Software's compact studio Reason. Admittedly, this program offers no audio tracks, but it *does* offer samplers, and for some users this might be enough. Furthermore, the ReWire interface allows you to use Reason and Ableton Live together, in which case Live will provide the audio tracks and Reason the instruments to provide a hybrid program every bit as powerful as a full-blown MIDI-plus-audio sequencer.

Modular programs such as NI's Reaktor and Cycling 74's Max/MSP can also be used on their own. Both applications offer a variety of modules by which you can construct any number of different musical environments, making a sequencer largely superfluous.

It all depends on your individual needs and preferences. Not only can you make all kinds of music with the Mac but you can make it in all kinds of different ways. With the Mac, designing your own music environment, mixing and matching software and devising your own ways of working can prove almost as creative as making music itself.

## Mixing At The Computer

As I mentioned earlier, a mixing console is used to combine the signals of different tracks, enabling you to adjust their volume, their positions in the stereo or surround image and their tone colour, and also to add effects. When it comes to these kinds of tasks, there's essentially no difference between a software and a hardware mixer.

Beware of generalising in this area, however; a Yamaha mixer isn't the same as a Midas console, and Logic's mixer is different from Cubase's and Ableton Live's. Nor is a mixer's functionality dictated by the software alone; the audio hardware and drivers also play a part.

### Channels, Tracks And Inputs

That said, however, regardless of the driver and the audio hardware they use, all software mixers offer multiple mixing channels, the exact number of which depends on the number of tracks available rather than the number of physical inputs. Each track in an audio sequencer requires a separate playback channel in the mixer.

The physical inputs on the audio hardware allow external signals to be recorded and integrated into the mix, but they're not confined to particular channels like they are on a hardware mixer. For instance, the same stereo input can be used for recording any number of tracks (although obviously not at the same time). The only limitation is on the number of channels that can be recorded simultaneously.

Each mixer channel is capable of delivering either the audio material already recorded on the track with which it's associated or, if the track has been record-enabled or its monitoring function activated, any input from an audio hardware device.

Not only is the number of channels independent of the hardware used, but so are the routing options within the software and the provision of busses. Every sound card offers at least one stereo output, which is normally assigned to the master buss for the purposes of monitoring.

**Audio channels or instruments can be routed to the master buss either directly or via a group**

As well as the master buss, there are other busses in the mixer to which signals can be routed. Obviously, if your audio hardware offers only a single stereo output, the signals from all of these busses will eventually flow into the master, but they can be very useful nonetheless. For example, if you've carefully balanced the various components of the drum kit but then decide that the entire set is too quiet, instead of having to move each channel fader and risk disturbing the balance, you can route the output from all the channels of the drum set to a single group. Then, when you move the group fader, it affects the entire drum kit as a whole, while the balance between the various instruments remains intact.

On the other hand, if your audio hardware offers additional outputs, these can be put to all kinds of uses. With eight outputs, for example, you could create both a stereo and a surround 5.1 mix or create a separate foldback mix for each performer, each tailored to give prominence to their own instrument.

### Effects And Instruments

As well as being able to control the volume level and pan position of each channel, most software sequencers also offer a number of other parameters and functions, with most programs having equalisers and sometimes dynamic processors, too. However, rather than offering a fixed set of functions in the input channels, most sequencers are designed to provide slots into which effects plug-ins can be inserted. Nearly all the software sequencers currently on the market come bundled with a selection of plug-ins, while there are also hundreds of plug-ins in various formats available from third-party developers.

As on a hardware mixer, with a software sequencer you can insert an effects processor directly into the signal chain of a single input channel (ie an *insert effect*, whereby the entire signal of that channel, and *only* that channel, passes through it) or you can make it available to all channels (ie a *send effect*, which is fed with signals from a separate buss taking varying amounts of each channel's signal, with the rest remaining in the channel itself). As a rule, then, an insert accepts all of the signal of a single channel, whereas a send effect accepts part of the signal of two or more channels.

Unlike a hardware processor, a plug-in can be used as many times as you like in various instances scattered around the mixer. However, each time you use a plug-in, it imposes an additional burden on the host computer's CPU. But as long as your system has enough power (and with a fully stocked G5 you should be able to run over 100 plug-ins at once), you can insert

multiple plug-ins in the same channel to create an effects chain.

You'll often find software synths and samplers in the form of plug-ins. Unlike effects plug-ins, these create audio signals rather than process them. Like their hardware counterparts, they generate audio signals in response to MIDI messages, so their input is MIDI while their output is audio. Other than that, they function like normal audio tracks – for example, they can be inserted into the signal chain after the tone generator, where they can be fed MIDI data from a MIDI track, while this track is being recorded. In live performance, the source is likely to be a MIDI keyboard.

### Automation And Recall

The mixers of all the larger audio sequencers offer two features called *total recall* and *automation*, which means that they allow you to record not only the static settings of all the parameters at various moments but also how you move the controls in real time as the song plays. For instance, if you push the fader of the sax channel at the start of the sax solo and pull back the fader slightly when the solo is finished, the same movements will be repeated each time the track plays back, with the fader moving as though under the influence of an unseen hand.

It's not just volume faders and pan pots that can be automated like this; you can also automate the knobs, switches and faders controlling the parameters of any effect or instrument plug-in that's currently loaded. Also, not only will they record your interaction with the controls in real-time but most sequencers enable you to edit the resulting data (displayed graphically) as well as draw in new automation data with the mouse. In this respect, data generated at the mixer is no different from performance data – it can be built up track by track and mistakes can be corrected at any time.

Although total recall is something that should never be taken for granted in a hardware mixer, it's almost universal in software mixers because the song document already contains all the data relating to the mixer settings, so whenever you save the document and close the application, the layout of the mixer, the routing, the channel assignment and the position of all the faders, knobs and switches are all stored along with the notes and controller movements. This means that, when you reload the song, all the knobs and faders are returned to their correct positions. A hardware mixer can only provide the same recall function through the use of motorised knobs and faders.

### Native And DSP-Based Processing

All the processing performed by a computer-based (ie digital) mixer imposes a burden on the host computer's CPU, and so its functionality is limited by the power of the computer.

While most modern computers have no problem with juggling volume and pan settings, or even with a judicious use of effects, if you use too many plug-

in effects and instruments you can overload the CPU. In such cases, one solution is to use expansion cards equipped with DSPs (Digital Signal Processors) capable of taking some of the strain by assuming responsibility for the processing needs of some or all plug-ins.

Some DSP-based systems go even further, dealing with the processing requirements not only of the plug-ins but also of the entire software mixer. Digidesign's Pro Tools is a classic example of this kind of system, although Creamware's Pulsar/Scope also offers the functionality of a DSP-powered mixer and imposes no burden on the host computer's processor. DSP-based mixers generally offer the least latency and so can outperform host-based systems when it comes integrating external signals into the mix.

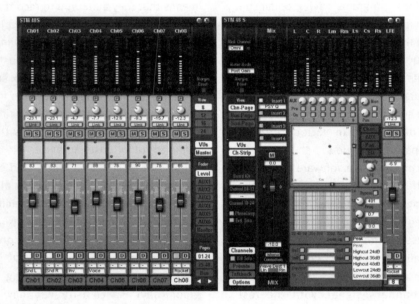

**The STM 48, part of the Creamware product range, which includes a variety of DSP cards and an extensive software package**

# Short Of Processing Power?

The day may come when your mouse pointer no longer moves smoothly across the screen and you begin to notice little clicks and timing irregularities during playback. These are the classic symptoms of CPU overload, and on encountering such problems you might find yourself wondering whether you'd be better

off buying a new computer or investing in optional DSP hardware.

While professional users with deadlines to meet might be able to reach for the chequebook, semi-pro and hobby musicians with less money to spend but more time to reflect should be able to come up with a more cost-effective solution.

## Slaves And Masters

Phrases like 'the virtual studio' tend to create a slightly unrealistic view of the capabilities of home studios, and this, combined with some users' inexperience with such systems, has led to many home- or project-studio-based productions snarling to a halt and a great deal of unnecessary frustration and disappointment.

While people who bought into the dream must have realised that there had to be some real-world limitations imposed on the virtual studio – that recording of vocal tracks might prove problematic in a flat that shakes every time a train goes by, for example – people seem to have swallowed the myth that, in the virtual world, all things are possible. Either that or that any shortcomings it did have could be removed by throwing money at them. Of course, when this turned out not to be the case, many people were disenchanted with the whole business of making music.

The blessing and the curse of a computer-based production environment is that it is an open system, and therefore there are no limits – at least, theoretically. At any rate, this is the general view held by most newcomers to the world of computer-based music, who then can't understand it when they come across obstacles they didn't think existed.

In a real studio, the limitations are physically obvious. You can tell at a glance whether the mixer has 8, 16 or 32 channels and that there's only one reverb or compressor. A software mixer, on the other hand, may boast an unlimited number of channels, and the sales blurb might convince you that you can use as many instances of each plug-in as you like. But it makes no difference whether the limitations are imposed by software or by hardware; the important thing to understand is that they exist in the first place.

Of course, our constant urge to overcome limitations and to push back frontiers is what makes us human, so these limitations can be viewed as a challenge. It's when there truly are no limitations – when the possibilities are endless – that people start to feel inhibited because, however well they succeed, they always feel as though they could have done better. We'd probably approach making music in a better frame of mind, and would probably find it more rewarding, if we used a little ingenuity and found a way of overcoming problems instead of upgrading our computers with DSP cards or replacing them with more powerful models every time we encountered them.

I'm not going to try your patience by saying things like 'You can make great music with nothing more than a mouth organ', or 'The Beatles produced great music with only three and a half tracks'; instead, I'll just point out that, throughout the ages, the vast majority of musicians have simply accepted their instruments as they were. If Paganini ever regretted that his fiddle wasn't as loud as an Alpine horn, it didn't stop him practising.

## Don't Upgrade – Downsize!

As with any other tool, in order to get the best out of the Mac you have to adapt the way you work to the way it works. No matter how intuitive software designers try to make their products, there are some recording engineers – the worst (but by no means only) culprits being those who learned their craft in studios – who remain blissfully unaware aware that the habits they acquired while working with hardware may no longer be appropriate in a virtual studio.

As an example, novices with no understanding of the buss principle tend to insert instances of the same reverb plug-in in every channel, even though the sound would be no different – and the processing overload considerably less – if they used a single instance of the plug-in as a send effect, which could then be shared between multiple channels.

Another mistake is to assign a separate channel to every shaker, triangle or rattle and to apply a different set of effects to each – a holdover from the days of the MIDI studio, when the outputs of a whole battery of tone generators were linked directly to the mixer channel inputs without first being recorded onto tape. If you try to adopt this kind of approach with an audio sequencer, you'll end up with an unmanageable number of tracks and you'll squander your computer's processing power, because the more tracks you have, the more inserts you're likely to need. In this case, less is definitely more.

This is why it's impossible to define categorically what counts as too little processing power and what is enough. It depends not only on the scope of the project but also on how efficiently the computer is used. Besides, when the resources of the system begin to run low, it's usually a sign of sloppy musical thinking or else a dearth of ideas. With music, just as with speech, if you can't express yourself succinctly, it's probably because you're not quite sure what it is you're trying to say. In most cases, over-elaborate arrangements disguise a fundamental lack of inspiration. Taxing your brain a little more usually means taxing your computer rather less.

## DSP Cards

In the event that you really do need more processing power than your computer is capable of providing, you might find salvation in the shape of a PCI card. Loaded with multiple DSPs, these can free up your Mac by taking over the responsibility for implementing effects and tone-generation algorithms.

By far the best known and most successful system to make use of DSPs is Digidesign's Pro Tools. The first ever such audio system on the market, Pro Tools was already offering professional audio editing when native (ie CPU-based) systems were still limited to four audio tracks with tinny-sounding equalisers. Digidesign pressed their advantage and marketed the system well, and today Pro Tools is well supported by software developers and is still in widespread use in professional circles. Similar systems from rival manufacturers have never enjoyed remotely as much success, some flopping miserably.

For some time now, however, native-based systems have been providing serious competition for DSP-based systems. The days of cheap-sounding EQs are over, the notoriously high latency of native systems has been reduced to acceptable limits, and these days there are native-based systems that are highly versatile and meet with the needs of professional users. The widespread use of interfaces such as VST sparked the development of a huge and varied selection of effects plug-ins and software synths for native-based systems. In fact, in terms of versatility, these days native-based systems are superior to DSP-based ones.

However, just because a DSP card is there doesn't mean it's actually going to streamline your system.

Usually it's only those plug-ins that were specially designed to make use of DSP cards that can tap into the additional processing power they offer, so unless you have enough of these to use in place of standard plug-ins, there's not much point in buying one. If all your plug-ins are native versions, the DSPs will just sit there. So don't look on DSP cards as a universal solution; they won't increase the performance of your computer's CPU, alter the buss rate, improve the graphic capabilities or speed up the data-transfer rate.

DSP cards are most useful when you have no way of increasing the power of your computer and can't afford to replace it, and also when they come with a host of high-quality, custom-built plug-ins. As well as those produced by Digidesign (www.digidesign.com), DSP cards and software have been developed by TC Works (PowerCore, www.tcworks.de) and Universal Audio (UAD-1, www.uaudio.com).

## The Mac Live

As mobile computers become more powerful and more affordable, they are beginning to be seen more often onstage. While desktop computers are generally at an advantage in the studio, with their large screens and expandability, in live situations iBooks and Power Books have the edge.

But what do computers do onstage? How are they used? Unlike synthesisers, computers have a whole range of uses and can take over various tasks in a live performance. This section demonstrates some possible applications and offers a few suggestions for a live setup.

### Playing Solo

First off, let's take a look at the situation where there's only one performer on stage. What he's playing is irrelevant; the same computer could serve just as well with experimental electronic music, dance, classical or folk.

Unless you're planning to screen a huge projection at the back of the stage with a video beamer, the people in the audience will have no idea as to what degree you're using the computer. You could be miming the entire performance with the computer playing back a CD, or you could be playing entirely live with the computer simply recording the gig. Even those in the front row won't be able to tell.

While there are many views about what actually constitutes a live performance, in this section I'll just be covering the various hardware and software configurations with which the performer can influence his arrangement or the overall sound in a live situation.

Of course, it's possible to transport your entire studio setup to the stage, substituting a more powerful amp and speakers for the studio monitors. You could then load each song in turn into the sequencer and play back the audio tracks and software instruments via the Mac's audio output and the hardware tone generators (ie synths and samplers) via the Mac's MIDI output. However, the difference between doing this and simply playing back a CD is moot.

On the other hand, if you're constantly changing your setup to adapt to the live situation, it's a little different. You might, for instance, be just muting individual tracks or groups, or you might be activating loops and modifying EQ settings and plug-in parameters in real time, which could be seen as being part of the performance.

To avoid having to load each song in turn when you're onstage, you just need to copy them all into a single file, inserting a few bars' rest between songs. And if there's more cheering between songs than you expected, all you have to do is press the Pause button and wait for the noise to die down.

Of course, using a synth onstage isn't without its hazards and is subject to many limitations; after all, MIDI-plus-audio sequencers were designed to replace the tape recorder, not to serve as tools for live performance. For this reason, you won't be able to access the parameters as quickly or as accurately as you might like. Furthermore, most sequencers' user interfaces are jam-packed with icons you'll never need onstage but which, if clicked by mistake, could ruin the entire gig – ie the Metronome's Record button.

It's almost impossible onstage to set up loops that repeat smoothly. While it's possible to start and stop loops without any hiccups on a modern sequencer, and while rough loop points can be input live with a reasonable degree of certainty, the interface is far from ideal. Getting the sequencer to jump from one part of the song to the next is easy enough, but what would be really useful is for the sequencer to finish the current bar first and *only then* jump to the new location. Unfortunately, this isn't a function offered by most studio sequencers.

Step forward Ableton Live, which is designed for live use and enables you, for instance, to trigger the playback of audio files of any length on the hard disk via MIDI or from the computer keyboard, compressing or stretching them in real time to fit the tempo of the song, enabling you to create arrangements spontaneously, live, by combining audio files. It can also record such arrangements, along with all the changes made to parameter settings during the performance, and you can then edit the recording later in the studio.

Emagic's Logic is also useful in live situations as it enables you to place and manipulate loop markers using keyboard shortcuts. Individual sequences or entire groups of sequences – including mixing and plug-in automation – can be controlled precisely from the keyboard via the Touch Tracks function and transposed at will. Of course, this function can only be used with MIDI, not audio.

As well as MIDI-plus-audio sequencers, there are other software applications that can be used by solo artists in live performance. Propellerhead's Reason, for example, and modular solutions like Reaktor can be used to tailor instruments and define access to them during live performances. However, while modular software might offer the greatest amount of freedom, using it to create your ideal performing setup requires knowledge and experience. On the other hand, some modular audio programs offer a large number of ready-made software instruments, which makes the task of setting up your system that much simpler.

**Ensemble Performance**
When there are two or three of you onstage with computers, some things become more complicated and others things become simpler. Rather than being solely responsible for the sequence of events, if you're interacting with other musicians who also have instruments and computers, the performance can end up being exciting and surprising – and not just for the

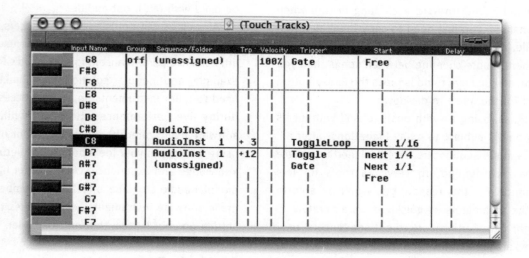

**TOP:** The clips in Ableton Live's Session view enable you to alter a song's arrangement in live situations

**BOTTOM:** With Logic's Touch Tracks function you can trigger sequences from the keyboard

audience; things can often go wrong, leading to impromptu variations in the arrangement. While knowing that this can happen might add to the rush of playing live, unless you pay careful attention to your fellow performers and exercise a little self-discipline when working with multiple computers, things can go more than just slightly wrong and the entire performance could descend into farce.

If you're using sequencing applications on multiple computers simultaneously onstage, they can be synchronised via MIDI clock. However, if one of you is just adding effects or playing a VST instrument from a MIDI keyboard, MIDI synchronisation is obviously no more necessary than it would be if he was playing a violin.

Even with two sequencers, it might not be necessary to synchronise them. As long as they're not both used for percussion (if one were supplying the kick drum and the other the snare, for instance, synchronisation would be vital) it might be enough to set both sequencers to the same tempo and start both machines on a signal.

Synchronising machines via MIDI clock works well but is a little complicated to set up. As well as hooking up the MIDI cables correctly, you have to decide which of the computers is to be the master and which the slave, and then you'll need to read the software manual to find out how to go about setting this up. (Most applications feature a dialog or menu item enabling you to assign master or slave status to the respective computers.) You could even hook up a separate device and use it as clock master, whose sole job is to generate clock signals, in which case both or all of the computers would be designated as slaves.

If you aren't using a dedicated time-code generator, the decision of which computer should serve as the clock master should be based on the roles played by the various computers during the gig. For example, if there's only one sequencer being used, the role of clock master should logically be assigned to it rather than, say, to a software synth running on one of the other computers and supplying only arpeggios. Of course, even the most logical choice isn't always the best one, so be prepared to experiment if you run into difficulties.

Whoever ends up using the computer assigned as clock master has considerable responsibility. Before each song starts, he has to check that the correct tempo has been set (and although this might seem obvious, this is a frequent source of frustration), that everyone is ready, that all the files have been loaded and that all the necessary parameter changes have been made.

**Live's Tap function provides great flexibility live. If the song is in 4/4, playback begins after the fourth tap**

The same goes at the end of the song. If the ending is predetermined, whoever's using the clock-master computer should check that the sequencer isn't in Cycle mode and that playback really does stop at that point, rather than looping back to the beginning, which could prove embarrassing. If it's an open-ended song with no definite ending, it's his responsibility to call a halt to the proceedings.

Of course, even though the MIDI clocks of the computers are perfectly in sync, their audio signals might not be, and this could be due to the fact that they have different latencies. As I explained earlier, latency is the time it takes for a computer to process the data involved in performing tasks – in this case, the delay between pressing a key and hearing the sound. If you're using several computers on stage and latency differences become noticeable, these latencies need to be harmonised, and this is generally done by adjusting the buffer size of one or more of the computers in the network in an attempt to find the lowest common denominator – ie the lowest latency with which all the computers in the system are capable of functioning without drifting apart.

Finding the lowest common denominator is only important if one or more of you are playing notes. If you're not doing anything that needs to be split-second perfect, you're best off erring on the side of caution and setting a fairly high latency value – perhaps as high as 50ms or 100ms – to make sure you don't overtax

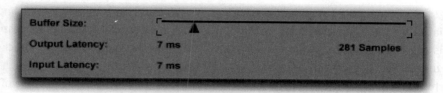

| Buffer Size: | | |
|---|---|---|
| Output Latency: | 7 ms | 281 Samples |
| Input Latency: | 7 ms | |

**Adjust the latency of your system by altering the buffer size**

any of the computers. However, if latency is a problem, the system can end up responding sluggishly to fader movements. Setting the latency to a value slightly above the lowest common denominator will reduce the risk of experiencing grating, clicks and dropouts, all of which are signs that the buffer size is too low.

Once you've established reliable system setup, don't be tempted to make changes just before a gig. Introducing new components can have unexpected and often drastic implications for the entire system. By all means upgrade your system from time to time, but do so in the practice room and try out the new configuration with all the songs in your repertoire before you venture out onstage.

## Audio Reproduction

If you haven't yet found or can't afford the right audio interface, the Mac's own audio output should be perfectly adequate for the purposes of live performance – especially if you have one of the later models, which output a surprisingly clean signal from their unassuming-looking mini-jack sockets. Be sure to set the maximum output level inside the computer rather than boost the volume later at the mixer or the output digital-to-analogue converter will be under-driven and you'll incur unnecessary signal degradation.

If there's hum in the system's audio signal, as is sometimes the case with the older generation of Power Books, try running your laptop off the battery instead of the mains; many of the PSUs (Power Supply Units) that come with Wall Street Power Books, for example, produce electro-magnetic interference that can contaminate the audio signal. To see whether or not it helps to hook up to the mains, stop playback, turn up the volume and listen very carefully as you pull out the mains plug. If the noise level drops, you'll know

that the PSU was the culprit. Sometimes it can help to change to a different PSU, preferably one that's better shielded.

If you're relying on the internal battery, you need to look carefully at your Mac's power-saving settings. After all, you don't want your computer going to sleep in the middle of a concert, and it can be embarrassing if the screen goes black or playback stutters because the hard disk keeps switching on and off in the middle of a song. To adjust these settings, select the Energy Saver icon (a lightbulb) in your System Preferences, then make the necessary adjustments on the Energy Saver panel.

## Assigning Roles

When you're performing in a band with multiple computers, each of you needs to be clear about who's doing what and what program you're doing it with. This is particularly important if you're using your computer's stereo output, as there may well be no independent monitor buss and it could become difficult to separate the output of your own computer from those of your bandmates.

When it comes to using combinations of programs live, there are so many variables that there's no point making concrete recommendations. What's best for you depends on what you want to achieve, your musical tastes and your budget. That said, you probably won't need to have a sequencer running on every computer; the main functions of an onstage sequencer are to host software instruments and to provide the basic framework for the live performance, but a single sequencer can usually cover both roles.

Of course, if your machine isn't running a sequencer, its processor is free to focus on other things, and this may well prove vital. When a computer is approaching its performance limits, it becomes sluggish and increasingly prone to crashing, and when the CPU load rises above 60% the computer becomes increasingly unresponsive. The lighter the load, the more responsive the computer becomes.

If possible, you're best off trying out the stand-alone versions of software synths instead of automatically using them as plug-ins. If a synth is equipped with an onboard step sequencer, you can usually integrate it into the network using just a MIDI clock signal. Of course, this limits you to a single instrument, whereas within a sequencer you could have several plug-in instruments running at once. And while it might be theoretically possible to play several virtual instruments at once onstage, in practice this isn't a good idea as having a bunch of windows open onscreen is distracting when you're trying to perform.

### Showtime!

Finally to an aspect of performing with the computer that has nothing to do with technology but is perhaps the most important of all. However swish your iBook or Power Book might look, it's never going to have quite the same visual impact as a full-on drum kit or a Marshall stack, and if you spend the gig staring at the monitor while fiddling around with the mouse, you're more likely to remind people of their accountants than Jimi Hendrix or Keith Moon.

Hanging your step sequencer around your neck and going walkabout like you're selling ice cream in a cinema is perhaps not a good idea, and hopping and skipping like a morris dancer with a gleaming Power Book in your hands would look absurd, but if you're hoping to entertain your audience, you must at least make an attempt to drop the 'drag' from 'drag and drop', as it were. Look committed. Stand rather than sit, and resist the temptation to light up or have a pint in the middle of the performance.

On more thing: If there are several of you working with sequencers, don't stare dumbly at the cursor as it crosses and recrosses the screen. You'll just look like you're watching a tennis match!

# APPENDIX

## Mac OS X On The Internet

The Internet is an important source of information, program demos, updates, shareware and sounds, all of which could help you to make music more effectively with your Mac. With this in mind, here's a list of websites of the companies mentioned in the course of this book, sorted by category.

## Sequencers And Major Programs

www.steinberg.de
www.emagic.de
www.ableton.com
www.propellerheads.se
www.native-instruments.de
www.motu.com
www.digidesign.com
www.cycling74.com
www.sagantech.biz
www.quadmation.com
www.bias-inc.com

## Effects Plug-ins

www.waves.com
www.pspaudioware.com
www.grmtools.org
www.prosoniq.net
www.smartelectronix.com
www.mda-vst.com
www.native-instruments.de
www.tcworks.de
www.sfxmachine.com

## Synth Plug-ins

www.native-instruments.de
www.steinberg.de

www.emagic.de
www.waldorf-gmbh.de
www.virsyn.com
www.refx.net
www.gmediamusic.com
www.arturia.com
www.bitheadz.com
www.ikmultimedia.com

## Sample Editors

www.tcworks.de
www.bias-inc.com
www.prosoniq.net
www.celemony.com
www.hairersoft.com
www.audacity.sourceforge.net

## Miscellaneous
### Sample CDs and CD-ROMs

www.bestservice.de

### CD Writers

www.roxio.de

### Music Notation

www.sibelius.com
http://debussy.music.ubc.ca/~opus1/
www.gvox.com

### VST To Audio Unit Conversion

www.fxpansion.com

### Audio Recording

www.ambrosiasw.com

**MIDI Hardware**
www.m-audio.de
www.edirol.de
www.novation.co.uk
www.doepfer.de
www.studiologic.net
www.evolution.co.uk

**Audio Hardware**
www.rme-audio.de
www.motu.com
www.m-audio.de
www.emagic.de
www.esi-pro.com
www.m-audio.de
www.edirol.de
www.presonus.com
www.yamaha.de
www.digigram.com

**DSP Hardware**
www.digidesign.com
www.tcworks.de

www.uaudio.com
www.creamware.de

**Information**
www.apple.com/downloads/macosx/audio/
www.macosxapps.com
www.osxaudio.com
www.harmony-central.com
www.kvr-vst.com
www.keys.de
www.keyboards.de
www.samplepool.de
www.amazona.de

**Worth A Look**
www.pete.yandell.com
www.grantedsw.com
www.plogue.com
www.creativedev.net
www.girl.yowstar.com
www.csounds.com
http://supercollider.sourceforge.net/
www.ircam.fr/equipes/temps-reel/jmax/en/index.php3

# NOTES